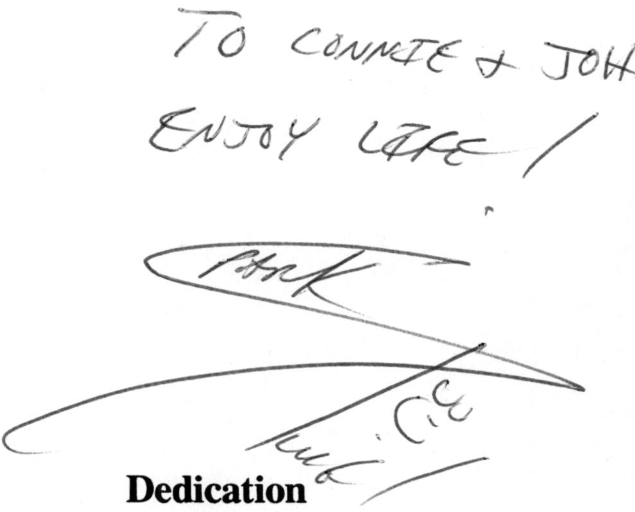

Dedication

To those who left the world too soon but whose *spark* remained to light the way for others.

Contents

Spark Plug

(spark plug) - 2. [Colloq.] n. a *person* who *inspires* or *energizes*.

A *spark plug attitude* is deeply rooted in the soil of commitment, persistence, faith, forgiveness, and the pursuit of excellence. It gives us raw courage to press through life's difficulties with unyielding determination.

Every champion exudes a *spark plug attitude.* The fruitless words, *"It can't be done"* do not rest on the tips of their tongues. They often risk *everything* to prove *"It can."* Even during the rough and stormy seasons of life, every beat of their heart faintly cries out, "I will *rise* again, *conquer* the impossible, and *sing* a song of victory!"

Deep in the recesses of every human soul, a mighty power is always at work. It serves as a constant reminder to achieve more, be more, give more and press onward.

Until we take the first step toward rearranging our lifestyle in a positive way, this mighty power will cause us to become as restless as a pregnant woman, held hostage by the piercing pain of intense of labor.

Giving birth to positive change will not come without shedding old habits, some old friends, and old ways of thinking. It will not come without tossing and turning, crying a river of tears, or lying awake in the still of the night beseeching God for answers.

***Answers** will come and **positive changes** will come. Though often wrapped in struggles and disappointments, torment and rejection, heartaches and pain, sickness and suffering, weeping and wailing . . . still, they come.*

- Jacqueline Thomas

Acknowledgments

We would like to thank the *unsung* heroes and heroines of our past for their written and spoken words of heartfelt inspiration. This book could not have come forth without all the brilliant ideas that have preceded ours.

We would also like to thank our parents, brothers, sisters, teachers, mentors, associates and strangers who continue to release a spark of encouragement into our lives.

Most important of all, we would like to thank God for being an anchor for our souls during the storms of life, a refreshing breeze of hope, and a keeper of His promises.

"A merry heart doeth good like a medicine: but a broken spirit drieth the bones."

— *Proverbs 17:22*

10 Ways to Spark Up Your Life!

1. Gratitude.

I am convinced that if we regularly take the time to count the blessings we *already* have, a fountain of jubilation will spring forth from the bottom of our souls.

2. Giving.

Giving to others sustains our 'usefulness' on this planet.

3. Enthusiasm.

Your inner zeal or passion has more power than you realize. Find ways to stir it up!

4. Faith.

Faith *ignores* facts. The antenna of belief is *always* positioned to *capture* the waves of possibilities.

5. Network.

No man can live wholly without the assistance or existence of another human being.

6.   Prayer.

Talking to God in prayer and giving Him enough time to talk to you provides energy and patience to endure the trials of life.

7.   Confidence.

When you believe you are the *only* person for the job, you accomplish half the task.

8.   Education.

Constant immersion in knowledge and the discipline to creatively apply what you learn will prepare you for untold blessings.

9.   Diligence.

A strong commitment to excellence in *all* your endeavors will definitely help you stand out from the crowd!

10. Forgiveness.

If you continue to deny mercy to those who have deliberately or inadvertently wounded you, undoubtedly the time will come when your own need for mercy will be *denied*.

PREFACE

You probably already know about the powerful and life changing impact that attitude has on the quality of your life. Its magnetic force will either pull you toward unspeakable joy and tranquility or cause you to plunge toward the depths of unending sorrow.

If you *haven't* discovered the awesome power of a *spark plug attitude,* a fantastic voyage awaits you as you begin to travel within these pages.

I believe the earth is longing to be sprinkled with more people who have *spark plug attitudes* or winning attitudes. The world has an unquenchable thirst for them because they are the ones who will boldly and triumphantly lead us into the next century. They are the ones who will not lose their deep and abiding concern for humanity in the midst of our technologically driven society. Undeniably, they are the ones who will continue to be our messengers of hope and beacons of light.

Our greatest fortunes are among treasures that cannot be physically touched, but you will never find *peace, joy, spark plug attitude, character,* or *unconditional love* listed as the most valuable assets of a Fortune 500 company.

Multitudes often spend a lifetime longing and searching for these rare jewels. However, the wonderful lessons of life teach us that inner peace, real joy, unconditional love, character and a good attitude cannot be bought, borrowed, or measured, and frankly, there are no substitutes.

Massive material success without a pleasant personality is like wearing a brand-new Armani suit with a pair of dusty, run over shoes. The shabby shoes spoil the whole suit. Similarly, a "poor attitude" instantly casts a wet blanket over all our accomplishments, no matter how *impressive* they seem.

Eyes, facial expressions and actions are the windows to our souls -- the windows that reveal how successful we *really* are. The way we treat other people, and even how we treat ourselves is an indication of the direction our moral compass is pointing.

The condition of our attitude is reflected by the condition of our inner being, or our *spiritual* house. When we *seek* to *grow* and mature *within,* our attitude will be transformed. Scales will fall from our eyes and doors will begin to open.

So as you begin to read this book, please don't let all the words become just another mental dish that you quickly gulp down and toss aside like an eight-course holiday meal. Savor and *apply* the principles that are *meaningful* to you. Your health, heart, mate, family, friends, co-workers and neighbors will thank you!

Jacqueline Thomas

Fayetteville, Georgia
January, 1999

Unveiling Your Treasure

Find a quiet place. Prepare yourself to be *inspired* and *renewed* as you begin to consume the words within this book.

We are about to take a stroll along the shores of life-- away from the raging sea of frustration and confusion that often cause us to lose our way and wander off the path of abundant life.

Along the shore, scattered here and there, you'll find charming seashells of *distilled* wisdom. You'll feel a *fresh breeze of inspiration* gently blowing through the corridors of your mind. You'll get a glimpse of a *sunny disposition* and experience a bit of humor. Inevitably, you will stumble upon words that will challenge you to change, encourage you to grow and anoint your soul.

We truly want you to look forward to receiving genuine encouragement that will enrich your life. So don't be surprised if we go to great lengths in order to help you unearth, polish and maintain your *spark plug attitude!*

If you have a little difficulty finding your treasure, you just might find it deeply buried beneath years of disappointment, resentment, pain, rejection, and a lousy self-image. (Hold on. Wait a minute. This is not a boring course in Psychology 101. Keep going!)

Attitude is built upon the foundation of our heritage, beliefs, fears, education, religion, experiences, hopes, and dreams. As we continue to mature, it becomes the nucleus of our very being. Just as we identify people by the color of their hair, skin or clothing, we also identify them by their *attitudes*.

My dictionary briefly defines attitude as a manner of acting, feeling or thinking that shows one's disposition, opinion, etc. In other words, our entire personality is made up of our thoughts, feelings, experiences and actions.

On the surface, *attitude* may seem like a trivial matter but it makes a big difference in the quality of our lives. It also determines the *depth* of our relationship with others.

Whenever we meet with someone, regardless of whether it is with our families, at work, church, social gatherings or school, our attitude will always leave a positive or negative impression. Quite often, the last thing people will remember about you is *your ATTITUDE*.

Think about it. After you have done all you can do in this world, it won't matter how masterfully the preacher or priest presents your eulogy, your attitude is the last thing everyone will remember. Every contribution you make toward encouraging or discouraging your fellow man is the fragrance that will endure in your absence.

The cornerstone of our attitude is really made up of what we *believe* to be true about ourselves. If our confidence is literally *dragging* on the floor, it is likely that we are being suffocated by envy, low expectations, silent frustration, and a lack of purpose.

Rarely will the 'unhappy majority' seek to grow. They often drag bulky, worn, outdated luggage behind them that is packed with painful childhood memories. This luggage is used as a scapegoat for every negative event that occurs in their life. No one can pry this burdensome luggage from their depleted souls. It must be *released*.

Each day *can* be a fresh slate, a new beginning, in spite of the past and in spite of all our frustrations. Though many opportunities have been sabotaged by yesterday's misfortunes, the past has no jurisdiction over our future. The past should only be used as a school for learning life's lessons and as a diary to record our triumphs.

Yes, it *is* a struggle to rid ourselves of painful remnants of grief, disappointments, and images of abuse that have etched themselves in our mind. It would be terrific if we could give our souls a thorough cleansing by simply erasing all the mishaps that occurred yesteryear or even yesterday. But there are no magic words that can do this for us.

Nevertheless, we can still be *determined* to find the *good* in *all* things, we can decide to forgive others *willingly*, and we can *carefully choose* where we let our thoughts dwell.

The cruelty we often encounter is not meant to be used as an excuse to remain in the valley of sorrow. There is a greater purpose for everything that happens in our lives. The traumatic experience in the valley is only meant to fortify our soul with wisdom, encourage us to become stronger, help us become more sensitive to the needs of humanity and eventually be used as a source of inspiration for others.

If we remain in the valley too long without recognizing the wisdom that can be gained, we will lose every shred of hope for a radiant and prosperous future. How can we boldly move forward if we are straining our neck to look back into our garbage heap of pain and disappointments with eyes of sorrow?

One of the most pitiful responses I've ever heard was from the person who whimpered, "But this is all I know to do, I don't know anything else. How do you expect me to know how to do anything else or act any other way?!"

In order for us to get to the next level, *we must begin to seek answers*. We can always find a *better* or *more excellent* way of doing anything we set out to do.

It doesn't matter where all the roads of cruelty and indiscretions have lead us in the past; miracles of restoration are still available.

So *today,* I want to speak to your life force and *command* you to live life to the fullest! *There's no reason to hold your head down, feel sorry for yourself or wander around without hope.*

Maintaining a spark plug attitude requires an appreciation for life's sacredness, *some respect* for humanity, a daily renewing of the mind, finding your purpose and some time set aside for fervent prayer. You will need faith to believe that your life will unfold as it should. A little patience is also required for pesky circumstances and difficult people that come to test your strength.

Every misfortune, misunderstanding, hurt, pain, etc., can either be methodically placed or hurled into an imaginary bonfire. It's not difficult. You just have to be willing. Casting it aside or kicking it to the curb is the only way to get some relief. As you begin to release excess baggage you will feel lighter and you'll soar higher!

The big question is . . . are you *willing* to let it all go, use it as a stepping stone and move on?

If not, you are in danger of living day to day without a vision for your life. You are in jeopardy of being tightly strapped in a straitjacket of self-pity, underachievement and depression.

My desire is to help you *stir up the gift* that is *already* within you and gently nudge you into becoming all that you were born to be.

Someone simply asked, "How tall will a tree grow?" and the simple response was, *"As tall as it can."* You were 'born to grow' into unimaginable heights in every area of your life.

Since the natural tendency for every living thing is to grow and improve, you cannot rest in the land of mediocrity *lest ye die*. Physical or spiritual death is the absence of abundant life.

Resist the urge to resign yourself to becoming one of the "living dead." You are *alive* and full of potential. You deserve to be here merely because you *are* here.

In our endless pursuit of seeking *'things'* to keep us warm, bring us comfort, or give us freedom, we find that we can never have enough. People, gadgets and toys eventually make us weary. We grow tired of them. Only the power of God can fill the cold and empty places in our hearts and bring peace to our soul.

Consequently, we come to realize that we definitely need to lean on Him in order to lighten our daily burdens. He is the *source* of all life, healing, encouragement, freedom, truth, joy, strength, creativity, and abundance.

What more can I say?

We don't claim to have all the answers nor do we expect you to embrace all that we share with you. However, one thing is for certain; you will definitely find one idea that's at least worth thinking about.

Brighter days will always await you. *So be forever encouraged. Refuse* to settle for mediocrity and keep on moving forward!

-Jacqueline Thomas

"After all is said and done, you will be remembered for your attitude toward others."

- Anthony B. Thomas

"The Spark Plug"

Chapter 1

"Change Your Attitude Young Man!"

The year was 1977. I was 13 years old - my first year as a teenager! It was also the first year I realized I had developed an "attitude problem."

At thirteen, no one could tell me anything!

"The Spark Plug" had *all* the answers or so I thought.

But then one day the intensity of my mother's words, which she had spoken so often, finally burned a hole in my heart.

"Change---your---attitude---young---man!"

I could no longer ignore these five simple yet powerful words. It was time for a positive change.

One beautiful spring day I decided to let an afternoon of tennis rescue me from the weekend routine at home. I could think better when I was battling it out on the courts. I was more focused. I thought if I tried hard enough, I just might be able to find a *quick* solution to my attitude problem.

While hastily gathering my tennis gear, I caught a glimpse of my mother standing at the kitchen sink. She was giving me the 'serious look'-- the look that always speaks louder than words.

I knew that was my cue.

Hurriedly, I made a dash for the front door.

"See you later mom. I'll make sure I'm back before dinner," I muttered.

I stumbled out into the gentle warmth of the sun. My rackets were awkwardly swinging over my shoulder inside my tennis bag. A feeling of exhilaration was slowly creeping upon me. I couldn't wait to get to the courts. It was a great day for tennis!

Though I tried to dismiss my mother's words, they continued to painfully echo in my ear and leave an annoying ache in my heart -- *"You need to change your attitude!"*

I began to wonder . . . "Now, what will it actually take to

change my attitude? What's the big deal anyway? Why is my mother always on my back about it? Why is this 'attitude' business making my mother fume? Better yet, how can I take control of something that seems so uncontrollable?"

I had no idea that I could *control* my attitude the way I controlled my backhand shot down the line on the tennis court.

Excuse Me, I Think Your Attitude Is Showing

We all live complex lives. It would be unrealistic to expect *anyone* to be jovial at every ticktock of the clock. No one should feel obligated to dance through *every* disappointment or stand up and cheer about the stress and strain of every burden. There are times when our trials and tribulations will totally knock us off our feet, snatch out our hearts and turn our world upside down. I've *never* felt like leading a cheering section during these times in my life.

For the record, having a spark plug attitude does not mean that we must wear a pasted-on smile, constantly have a toothy grin or walk around with a permanent halo over our head. It does not require us to get into the habit of allowing others to use us as a doormat. Humility has its place.

A spark plug attitude means . . . we have confidence that our life is *unfolding* as it should. It's showing respect for others who occupy space on this earth. It means standing our ground and fighting for our dreams despite rejections and fears. It means standing up for those who cannot stand up for themselves. It helps us to peel back the layers of each day and find a pearl of goodness in *every* situation.

A spark plug attitude ignites our hearts with hope and helps us stay in the race!

Whether it's good, bad or indifferent, wherever you are right now, your attitude is showing.

When you treat someone differently based on their appearance, your attitude is showing. When you pick a certain style of clothing over another, your attitude is showing. When you choose to surround yourself with a cloud of dismay, your attitude is showing. Even the simple decision to eat certain foods *reflects* your attitude.

Attitude and the *decisions* we make often share a common thread. More often than not, it is our *attitude* that governs the *choices* we make for our future.

It's important to talk about the *'power to choose'* because our place in life at the moment has been primarily made up of a series of choices. And whether we believe it or not, we are held accountable for each one we make. I ran across a Japanese proverb that said, "The reputation of a thousand years may be determined by the conduct of one hour." How true.

The power to choose is awesome. When we fail to make decisions that will somehow richly and positively fertilize our lives, we have automatically made a choice not to richly and positively fertilize our lives. Until we accept the fact that *we* are most often our own stumbling block, we will *never* move forward, see beyond our circumstances, or prosper. The firmly anchored walls of disappointment, defeat, and regret, that overshadow us are often crafted by the choices we've made.

Even if . . . someone uses brutal force upon you, you're falsely accused of a crime, involved in some kind of accident, born with physical challenges, or encounter other situations that are beyond your control, you are the person who will *execute* the master program for your life. In the face of all these things, you will still be left with the power to choose. You still have the power to choose to either *drown* yourself in sorrow or *live* in victory!

Some of you may be saying, "I'm stuck in a rut and disgusted with my life."

Well, what's really stopping you from moving forward? Who instructed you to give up, sit down, and manufacture a sour outlook on life?

I once met a homeless man whose wife had been unfaithful to him. "It's all her fault," he complained. "On top of that, she divorced me and took everything," he added.

"How long have you been divorced?" I asked.

"Twenty years," he said with a faraway look in his eyes.

He was still holding his wife responsible for his homeless condition. Twenty years of his life had been frittered away and he was in danger of wasting many more.

If you think your 'dreadful' past is holding you back, I believe you are shamelessly denying the present and brazenly disrespecting the future. If you claim a certain person is holding you back, then you haven't begun to understand the creative, intelligent, uniquely talented and gifted person that you are. Without a doubt, you have a purpose for your life and the only person that can keep it from you is sitting in your seat.

If you are afraid of looking foolish, stumbling or falling in your quest for a better quality of life, just remember that character producing experiences are necessary for growth.

Speaking of a better quality of life, I recently discovered that my mother went back to finish school at twenty-one years of age.

A series of heartbreaking events had interrupted her education.

Divorced from an abusive husband and having the responsibility of three small children, she set out to construct a better future for us as well as herself.

Determined to succeed, she faced the humiliation of other high school students, five and six years her junior, by going back to the 10th grade at the age of twenty-one.

My mother graduated from high school. She went on to college to receive her undergraduate degree as well as her Master's degree. Diligently, she planted seeds of sacrifice and overcame the obstacles that had once held her hostage.

Some of you may contend that your lack of education is holding you back. "If only I had finished college or even gone to college, I would have a better chance of reaching my goals" some may grumble. This statement may or may not be true for everyone. It depends on what your goal happens to be.

A good education is as essential as oxygen. Educating ourselves from the time we are born until we exit this earth is mandatory. However, the best education does not always come *entirely* from the laboratory within the confines of university walls. The local library is still a complimentary gold mine that is saturated with valuable and intriguing information. Our experiences are also exceptional teachers and training is available on every topic imaginable.

The point I am tactfully trying to make is most people have fabricated a horde of excuses for not moving forward. These excuses help pardon them from feeling guilty about their lack of progress.

They believe they can escape the piercing eyes of others by blaming someone else. Blame weakens their power to make positive changes. It gives them an excuse for not taking responsibility for their actions. Yet, *blame* can never erase the years that have been carelessly traded for a life of inertia.

No Time to Whine

For some of us, being sincerely thankful for the gifts we already have is as rare as seeing a shooting star. It's so easy to forget or overlook the little things that mean so much.

It was Shakespeare who declared "Happiness is not having what you want, but *wanting* what you have."

The World Bank recently reported that about *1.3 billion* people on the planet get by on less than $1.00 per day. *Less than one single dollar!*

Can you imagine getting by on that much?

Well, let me make these statistics a little more meaningful.

There are about 260 million people in the United States. So, 1.3 billion is equivalent to multiplying all the people in the United States by five. If you don't have a wall size map of the U.S., get one and place it on your wall or lay it out on the floor. Study the map for a moment, try real hard to imagine 260 million, then multiply it by five. The harvest of people who would be delighted to have a fraction of your opportunity is staggering!

Compared to their own financial situation, *one out of every five* people in the world could classify you as being in the same financial category as Donald Trump or Oprah Winfrey.

We take too much for granted. We constantly sob, whimper and whine about not being able to satisfy our ego. In a rich land of endless opportunities, we make too many excuses.

Stop right now and find a pen and a sheet of paper. Take a few moments to identify the phantoms in your life that are stopping you from moving forward. Just think for five minutes or less.

Now jot down what and who they are. Then write in full detail how they are hindering you from progress. Be honest. There is no reason for you to hold back or be ashamed. This brief yet important exercise is for your eyes only.

Now, look closely at what you have written. Analyze every

excuse. Is there enough power on that sheet of paper alone to keep you from your purpose? Do you hear voices yelling from the paper demanding that you stay where you are and not move forward? Are powerful hands tightly locked together like a steel chain on that sheet of paper forming a barricade to hold you back? I don't think so.

If you still think others can keep you from your purpose, then you have been deceived. If you believe you cannot rise up from where you are and move on, you have been misinformed. You are *already* gifted with each and every attribute that is necessary for reaching your goals. It is your responsibility to *develop* them by getting wrapped up in the art of "doing." In other words, take action.

Nothing can stop you from doing what you were sent to this planet to do if you truly believe it. There is no excuse for having a stagnant, unproductive life that lacks growth and creativity.

Nothing can hold you back. Victory has been *engraved* in your past, present and future. The words 'ABUNDANT LIFE' have been stamped across your heart! You are an important piece to life's puzzle. Your solitary contribution is vital. All of the creation is screaming for you to complete your task!

Your children, grandchildren, cousins, nephews, and nieces are counting on you to complete your commission because they need to stand on your shoulders. The whole universe is cheering you on in this race with monumental banners that read, *"You can make it if you try. Please don't give up yet!"*

It may not be easy as one, two, three for us to find where we *fit* in this great big world but it is certainly our responsibility to stay alert for clues. In the meantime, just do your absolute best in whatever you are doing at the present. You have a grand design and a purpose for your life that will greatly impact the lives of others in ways you could never fathom!

It doesn't matter what is randomly thrown in your path, you can conquer it. You are an overcomer and you were born to overcome every single obstacle that comes your way. As the ambitious ant completes its mission of gathering food for the icy cold winter, you can complete your mission. The tiny ant takes one faithful step at a time, one morsel of delicate food at a time and slowly builds a warehouse of nourishment.

Yes, *timing* is crucial. I have painfully discovered and accepted the fact that divine order has its own built-in time table. There is nothing you can do to force it to operate. Scientists cannot force summer to come immediately after winter. We must first experience the pure essence of spring.

Before grapes can become a vintage wine, preparation is

completed and then the critical 'timing' element is set in motion. There are times when you just have to wait. But you must also *work* while you wait.

You must also be prepared. Every incident that occurs in your life is preparation for the next event. Someone once proclaimed, "It is better to be prepared and not have an opportunity than to have an opportunity and not be prepared." Every single circumstance that is allowed to come our way has **OPPORTUNITY** written all over it.

Your breakthrough may be wrapped in something you absolutely abhor or some tragic experience but you will never discover it if you are swimming in sorrow or criticizing the package. It's not easy to unwrap these kinds of packages. Pain usually surrounds each one of them. But after a certain level of maturity and growth is achieved, you will understand the lesson that each one contains and use it as a stepping stone.

The Axe Doesn't Have to Fall

Unfortunately, there are individuals who have literally given all their power over to other people, things, habits, situations and circumstances. That which controls them will often dictate how they walk and how they talk, the way they wear their hair, the style of clothing in which they adorn themselves, even down to the food they eat.

There are countless who have literally found themselves trapped in relationships which involve physical and verbal abuse. Everything started out just fine, but slight changes began to occur -- an insult here and there, a bruise every once in a while. Before long, it becomes the order of the day.

"Oh, he didn't really mean it, " becomes the parrot response to those who are bold enough to inquire. *"He just had a bad day at work.* Besides, *it was all my fault. He told me he was sorry and wouldn't do it again. "*

Night after night the victims lie in bed with their faces buried in a pillow, wet with tears. Eventually it becomes difficult to hide the bruises that have been inflicted. But there are also bruises that others will never see; they are mental and emotional. These are the bruises that tend to create barriers to real happiness and fruitful relationships.

I will never forget the portrait of neglect, sadness, and regret that were in the eyes and faces of the women at the shelter where I was a volunteer. Most of them had to flee with the clothes on their backs. Their small children were already acquainted with fear and violence. I'm sure if I had interviewed them five years earlier, they would not have predicted the trauma they would narrowly escape.

Most people are afraid of what they will lose if they leave. I am more concerned about what they will lose if they stay.

Don't wait for the axe to fall. *Please* don't ignore the signs of abuse! *Help is available everywhere.*

Once we give our power away, it diminishes and alters the valuable and unique person we were designed to be. Eventually, we begin to spill the energy which was originally meant to make a positive and lasting impact on the universe. Inevitably, we find ourselves ranked among the countless number of people who move as if they are sleepwalking--lacking the *will* to make a positive contribution.

Imagine losing a portion of your physical 'self' bit-by-bit until one day you cannot identify who you are anymore. Every day, an essential piece is missing. This is virtually what happens to the real essence of 'you' when others gradually steal your identity. All of your talents are discarded and you become a mere puppet on life's stage until the curtain comes tumbling down to signify "the end."

Those who seem to sit around and wait for the proverbial axe to fall before they take action all tell a similar story. (One day they 'woke up' and found themselves in their dismal situation.) It didn't happen overnight. It occurred slowly like years of erosion gradually melting a mountain into a heap of dirt.

After hitting rock bottom, rhetorical questions are asked such as: "What can I do to get out of this situation? How did my life come to this? God, why are you letting this happen to me? "

Hitting rock bottom is a blessing. Life is telling us to change our lethal lifestyle, stop letting our poison past control us and modify our toxic relationships or we may not live to see the light of day.

James Allen maintained that "Circumstance does not make the man, it reveals him to himself." We cannot stand at the spiritual gate, inspect every circumstance, and give it a stamp of approval before it comes into our lives. However, every circumstance *can* help us gather a few more nuggets of wisdom and develop strong character.

Soak Your Mind in a Tub of Inspiration

While writing this book, I began to really think about the power and capacity of the mind and how it can operate either as a friend or adversary. I also thought about the feeling of electricity that gently flows through our veins when the mind is genuinely refreshed. The *only* way I know of keeping the negative monsters at bay is by renewing the mind daily.

When the mind is renewed, it is similar to the *peace* that creeps upon you and caresses your soul as you're staring out at the timeless beauty of the deep blue ocean. It's like the *rugged confidence* of majestic mountains that stand tall in the midst of raging storms. A renewed mind promotes *healing* in the body as well as the soul.

I know sometimes we feel powerless when it comes to controlling our thoughts. They can be as dangerous as a runaway train.

Most often, before we are even aware of what has happened, in the vestibule of our minds, we have slaughtered things which should have been held sacred. We have torn the hearts of others to pieces and thrown it into the mouths of hungry wolves to be spewed out as fiery gossip. We have banished others from our presence because we didn't approve of the way God fashioned them.

We quickly degraded them because their vocabulary didn't exactly match ours or their subjects and verbs failed to agree. We probably also dismissed them because their apparel wasn't expensive enough, they didn't have enough money or just didn't rank high enough on the 'people with power and prestige' scale.

It's normal for a bull to start running and destroying everything in its path because that's what a bull does. But what about the proverbial bull that's always running around in your head? Does it also attempt to destroy everybody and every thing or are you training it to be on good behavior by renewing it daily?

There are no magic formulas for a spark plug attitude. But the *process* can begin at the moment you decide to do something about it. Yes, it's important to read books on a daily basis that inspire you; however, a change of heart will never occur from *just* reading a book. Reading the book can only condition your mind. Opening the door of your heart is another matter.

People may temporarily change because the information is at the forefront of their minds, but when the knowledge is forgotten, the same old habits emerge. Again, the mind must be renewed daily in order for the heart to remain sensitive to change. When our heart really becomes hardened, positive words from a book or the powerful words of others cannot easily penetrate it.

So what must you do? Apply, apply, and reapply information and thoughts to your mind that are healthy and wholesome. Write out a memo to yourself about YOU -- your value to yourself, your family and society. Let it be filled with all of your wonderful attributes. (I'm sure you have some.) Include your goals and aspirations. Read the memo to yourself regularly. It will boost your natural energy and enthusiasm!

Read, read, and read again inspirational material. Post uplifting quotes around your home or at work. Find photos of family, friends, vacation spots or bright and colorful pictures of nature and have them enlarged. Try to place them around areas where you spend most of your time. Listen to music that will lift your spirit. Find a hobby that excites you. Set aside time to enjoy life!

For the record, I didn't stumble upon any answers that beautiful spring day when I decided to flee to the tennis courts. Nevertheless, it was the beginning of a life of seeking, growing, stumbling and falling that brought me to where I am today.

The ability to posses and exercise a 'spark plug attitude' is still one of my creeds for living an abundant life. I've accepted the fact that I'm not perfect. Sometimes I'll run completely out of fuel. Yet I will continue to welcome the challenge of maintaining a spark plug attitude again and again and again. I will continue to accept the challenge of giving hope to a hurting world.

SPARK PLUG
POINTS TO PONDER

1. Wherever you are right now, your attitude is showing whether it's good, bad or indifferent.

2. Until we realize that we are most often our own stumbling block, we cannot mature, and we cannot begin to change.

3. Every incident that occurs in your life is *preparation* for the next event.

4. We cannot keep circumstances from coming, but we can certainly find out who we are, and where we need to go because of them.

5. In some ways hitting rock bottom is a blessing. It forces us to come to the crossroads of life and make positive decisions about where we would like to go.

"It is a funny thing about life; if you refuse to accept anything but the best, you very often get it. "

- Somerset Maugham

Chapter 2

A Celebration of You!

Not only does a celebration of your identity involve the miracle of *how* you made it here, it also includes your fascinating journey *while* you are here.

I have never met a woman whose egg was fertilized on a given day and *ShaZAM,* the precious little bouncing baby girl or boy appeared lying in the crib on the next day.

You are not here by accident or because God suddenly had a moment to spare and penciled you into his appointment book. You are truly a masterpiece, a beautifully written song, a blazing star in the night, a gift for all seasons!

The pattern for your unique skills, abilities, knowledge, gifts and talents were delicately written in your mother's womb. Imagine being a blueprint somewhere in the universe even before your physical arrival. Absolutely amazing, isn't it?

Quickly, nature pulled back yet another royal silk spiritual curtain when you made your grand entrance. God allowed an additional *gift of life* to arrive on the scene and announce its debut into the world!

Nature wasn't concerned about what you looked like or whether you liked the color green, yellow, gold or blue. It wasn't concerned about whether you would like spinach or had the vocal ability to sing like a songbird. When you came out kicking and screaming, nature understood a 'human being' had won the privilege of breathing the air and contributing the gifts and talents that were deposited in them.

Nature understood that the sacred appointment was set for *you* and nothing could change it. The entrance fee was already paid. And now, here you are reading a book that was part of my blueprint in *my* mother's womb!

Believe it or not, if you do not appreciate and make peace with yourself, it is almost impossible to wish the best for someone else. If you do not take the time to lavish healthy love upon yourself, it is very *unlikely* that you will freely pour love upon your children or other people around you. If you haven't discovered that your presence on this earth has been ordained by someone GREATER than man, you'll always believe your destiny has been placed in the hands of mortals.

Nobody Knows How Much My Heart Hurts

Those who have crippled hearts and broken spirits cannot comprehend the depth, breadth and intensity of the gnawing pain that they inflict upon others. Their silent scream for help is manifested as a whip that unmindfully and unmercifully beats upon the feelings and emotions of people around them. The real tradgedy is that too often some of them *turn* on themselves.

The Centers for Disease Control reported that in 1995 suicides (31,284) exceeded homicides (22,552). It has been said that every 15 minutes a person commits suicide in the United States.

Though every situation is different, I am convinced that many who commit suicide despise themselves so deeply that they can no longer coexist with the person they have *imagined* themselves to be. They no longer find life meaningful and literally become *suspended* in an 'awful' world that is lonely, cold, wicked and meaningless. They feel as if they have practically lost control of everything and some just want the *pain* to stop. Internal *emotional collapse* will eventually cause them to rid themselves of themselves. Material goods are not enough to mend the torn fabric of their broken lives and wounded souls.

I am inadequate. I am stupid. My parents are ashamed of me. I never get anything right. I'll never be able to do thus and so. I am worthless. I am so lonely. I wish I could have lived my life another way. Nobody cares about me. I can't lose this weight. My mother abandoned me. Everybody is always picking on me. Everyone is out to destroy me. Why did my dad leave me and why won't he ever call? I'll never be able to get out of this financial mess. Why is this happening to me?!

Fatalistic thoughts seem to constantly hover over the sad souls who snuff out their lives. They lose all hope and submerge themselves in a pit of worthlessness. More often than not, they can only hear the blaring voices of those who *belittle,* not the powerful words of encouragement that are so rare. Somehow they are convinced that their world is the *only one* that is crashing into smithereens.

Depressing? Sure. However, the reality of this situation remains the same . . . too many people slosh around in this negative pool too often.

None of us have all the answers. None of us are perfect nor will we ever experience a perfect life on this earth. We are constantly in search of something or someone that will make us complete and keep us content. But somehow the search always lead us right back to ourselves.

Our greatest desire is to be free on the inside. We want the security of knowing that someone genuinely loves us as we are. Sometimes a whole lifetime is required to work out the kinks that cause us to become internally bound.

Sadly enough, the suicide survivors, the lives that are left behind suffer tremendously. They are left with no real closure, no real answers and no relief. Just as they struggle with the guilt of not being able to identify someone else's pain, they also wallow in the guilt of not being able to get through to a human heart that was hurting so much.

A Day at A Time

Because our vision is so limited, we never know how the story of our life will end. If we don't stay until the *curtain falls,* we just might miss a powerful and awesome scene. You *never* really know how things will work themselves out! All things really work out for the good and are used for the good in the end.

I still believe the joy we are capable of experiencing in this life is in direct proportion to the sorrow and pain we are able to walk through. Anyone can hold on for just one more day!

So often we underestimate the *needs* and the *value* of just being human. We forget that we are connected in ways we cannot imagine. We need each other in order to survive. We are all companions riding along in the same ship (earth). Everyone cries out for a little civility in some form or fashion.

Scientists have proven that babies will actually die if they are not held enough. We desperately *need* the transference of unconditional love and concern from one to another. Unfortunately, it is only during times of tragedy that we can get a glimpse of this phenomenon.

The real issue of suicide *often* lies in being totally consumed with 'self', i.e., *your* wants, *your* needs, *your* problems, *your* pain, *your* "shortcomings" or *your* disappointments.

Volunteer some time to be with those who are less fortunate, it has an interesting way of changing your perspective and trivializing *everything* that ails you.

I have extraordinary talent! God . . . He who keeps the earth spinning on its axis and rules the universe with authority is always present in times of sadness, sickness and rejection. He is present in joy, health and happiness. He is present when I am alone and He is present in a crowd. He is present when I am awake and when I am asleep. He is present in the fires of life and when the breeze of peace gently covers me.

I was born to triumph in all things. No one else has all the tools to carry out the mission that I was sent to this world to do. I can spread the perfume of love wherever I go. The world really needs me because the humanity department has a shortage of goodness and mercy. This day, I choose to live. I will become aware of the love, life, sights and sounds that surround me and give thanks!

Try saying these things aloud more often and believe it!

If you faithfully picked up the pieces of your dream from where you are, you can still complete your assignment. Every day is a crisp new page in the story of your life. What memories will you write on the pages of your existence today?

Whatever you've experienced or whatever decisions you've made, they are all still wrapped up in your destiny to be great. Nothing is ever wasted. Life will gladly be your number one tutor in spite of the choices you make. In spite of the pain that was inflicted upon you, something of value can still be extracted from every degree of chaos.

Danger Zone

If one of your friends or associates could describe your attitude in a few words, what would those words be? Have you ever tried to see yourself as others see you? Who or what does the world see when you walk by in the parade of life?

OK, OK, maybe it doesn't matter to you what the world sees. But what about your children and the other family members that you represent-- what is their perception? What kind of influence or impression are you making on them?

At times we behave in a manner in which we are not usually aware. We don't always know when we are moving toward the danger zone. Sometimes someone else has to point it out to us. We need others to remind us to keep our feet on the ground.

Dear God,
I Don't Wanna Be Me!

I heard Leo Buscaglia proclaim that in all of his many years of teaching, when his students were asked if they could be anyone in the world, who would they choose--the majority always chose someone else. Few of us are really satisfied with the physical qualities or talents and gifts that we have. No matter how talented we are, there is still a hunger in our souls to have *more* talents. This is interesting because usually we don't exercise the talents we *already* have. What are you doing with yours?

Remember, *you* are the most incredible and glorious achievement under the Milky Way! You have something so powerful, so electric and so valuable to contribute that no one else can bestow it upon the world but you. It may be your keen mind, precious parenting skills, healing smile, awesome creativity, melodious voice, gifted hands, or magnetic personality, but whatever it is, it's valuable!

Decorate Your Soul

What attributes are you waging a war against . . . your face, physique, etc.? We keep mistaking the real essence of beauty as something tangible or something the eyes can behold. How long will we remain in battle with ourselves, distorting our own image?

We make sure we are presentable on the outside while cobwebs of unforgiveness, fear and hate are as thick as a cotton blanket on the inside. Real gold lies within the hills, not on mountain peaks for everyone to get a good look. The true essence of beauty *still lies within.* (It's not just something 'ugly' people say.)

Looking on the outside is too simplistic. For a moment, just imagine that you've decided to buy an exquisite home in a quiet, upscale neighborhood by merely inspecting the outside. The home looks as if it's a castle built for a king. The emerald green landscape is flawless and the shrubbery is carefully chiseled by the hand of a master designer.

An assortment of fragrant flowers of every hue are in bloom all over the priceless property. Daffodils, rhodendrons, azaleas and daylilies dance in the wind. A fully stocked pond with crystal clear water will suit the amateur who loves to fish. A large in-ground pool with an artistic design is in the back of the residence. Two magnificent golden lions guard the entrance and the circular drive is lined with hand-carved lamp posts shipped all the way from Paris. The upgraded amenities outside of the castle are just too numerous to mention.

After you paid your hard-earned money and wandered inside the house, you suddenly realized it was gutted out by termites and infested with rats and other loathsome pests. Cheap paint was peeling off the walls and a whole side of beef was left on the kitchen counter in a decomposed state. You couldn't tour the whole house to assess damages because the unpleasant odor, uninvited pests and ragged interior drove you away.

You wanted to get out of the deal but you had signed the contract that demanded you remain there until another buyer was found.

I wonder how many relationships turned out this way. A bad attitude, complete with horns and claws emerged as soon as you thought you had fallen in love with your beauty queen or handsome prince. Before you classify something or someone as beautiful, make an effort to find out what's inside first.

Are you attempting to walk in someone else's shoes by studying their every move?

You won't begin to experience fulfillment until you walk in your own purpose. Life does not deliberately play games with us to keep our calling hidden. We usually cannot discover our purpose because our minds tend to zoom in on what we *do not* have rather than what we have. You'll be amazed at the things that happen when you begin to operate in the gifts and talents you already possess. If you're still trying to figure out what your gifts and talents are, just take a poll from people that know you.

I believe as we enter the great Judgement, God will literally ask us, "Why didn't you do more with your life? Why didn't you become all you were born to be? Why did you consistently covet your neighbor's gifts, talents and other attributes while neglecting to multiply your own? Why were you always feeling sorry for yourself? Why didn't you look in your own mirror? Why, why, why?"

We are always looking from the corner of our eye at other people to measure ourselves by them. The grass is always healthier, prettier and greener over the fence or in the other yard. We continue to revel in this and before we realize what is happening, our own fruitful lives have become spoiled. One by one, our dreams begin to fall to the ground like dead leaves from a tree. Our energy fades like a rainbow after a refreshing shower of rain. Unproductive years eventually transform themselves into painful wreckage of our past.

So, have you given your voice away, attempting to sound like someone else? What about your weight, are you literally *dying* to look like someone else? Has materialism taken you hostage so that you can only imitate life while leaving your soul without substance? Have *you* fallen into the trap?

Attitude: A Condition of The Heart

At this point you may still be wondering why attitude is getting so much fanfare. After all, you may know a host of people who are 'successful' with a bad attitude. They seem to have the Midas touch. No matter what they decide to do, it prospers. But *character* and the external trappings of success don't always walk hand-in-hand.

Even though an individual may be financially secure and successful with material gain, this same person may be destroying their health or sacrificing valuable relationships. This is *hardly* an illustration of prosperity.

In a material and spiritual sense, there are two kinds of success -- good success and bad success. A cloud of 'bad success' will eventually surround people whose empire has been built by walking on the backs of others to "get ahead."

The creatures of bad success constantly use all kinds of schemes and tricks to accomplish their goals. They *always* look out for number one and the sum of their possessions will usually define who they are in the "*status-sphere.*"

In the end, the people with 'bad success' worry day and night about losing the 'good fortune' they have been so careful to hoard away.

"Who cares?!" are their famous last words when friends are lost. Slowly, their identity becomes buried in everything they take into ownership. Somehow they believe they can 'get along' without support from others.

This negative brand of success will cause health problems which leave the doctor clueless. Family obligations are often neglected in exchange for one more sale, closing one more business deal or making one more acquisition in order to climb to last rung of the corporate ladder. Often, the heroic milestones in the lives of their children go unnoticed.

Bad success often finds these victims all alone with no one to share their accumulated wealth and no one to love. They often learn too late that everything was all a mirage and they missed out on the main *reason* for living-- *to grow to give and to love.*

Those who expect good success help others along the way because no one really makes it alone. Generous contributions are made to society. Enough time is taken for much needed rest and relaxation. Preparations for the future are made and life is lived to the fullest.

Quality time is also set aside to spend with family and loved ones. Values and morals are instilled in the children. Instead of allowing material possessions to define their level of success and who they are, they simply enjoy them and act as temporary caretakers. Good success is often crowned with a winning attitude.

Attitude can determine what job you will have, whom you will marry, whom you will divorce, where you will live, how much money you will make and so forth. It will determine how you are represented in this life.

Are you a person of values, morals and integrity? Or are you a ruthless dictator with a desire to only satisfy yourself? I think you know the answer.

Why not give yourself an attitude checkup? I've heard that the biggest room in the world is the one for improvement. We all could greatly benefit from a little refinement. Control your attitude, or it will control you.

Taming the Tiger

So why do so many of us have difficulty trying to keep the attitude dragon at bay? What makes us give all our power over to our emotions? What makes us hold on to the negative images in our mind while allowing the positive ones to flee?

We often wrestle with staying cool, calm and collected when we would rather *fly off the handle*. But what does it really solve? Are we more mature after we finish yelling at the top of our lungs? Have we really gotten it off our chest? Did we really *solve* the problem that was tormenting our spirit? After we called someone a few obscene names did we somehow feel better?

Maybe, maybe not.

These are all questions with answers which often elude us. We are creatures with turbulent emotions, a whirlwind of activity is going on in our brains at this very moment. Getting to the origin of why we do certain things and explaining the often twisted path is almost impossible. Experts declare heredity is the culprit for most of our actions. Others maintain that we lack a healthy portion of "emotional intelligence."

Nevertheless, you are the keeper of your own heart. It can be a beautiful well-kept garden both vibrant and picturesque or it can be like an untamed forest with wild weeds, broken branches and hollow trees. Just as it requires time and discipline to create a beautiful landscape from untilled soil in the wilderness, it may take time and discipline for you to *completely* set your winning attitude free. Your liberation is in direct proportion to the amount of negative baggage you are willing to release.

Change is difficult because we make it so. For most of us, letting go of comfort or old ways of doing things is as difficult as getting Linus (Charlie Brown's sidekick) to give up his torn, soiled blanket. This false security can become a way of life. Change is your choice -- your decision. If you want to dig your way out of your own grave, you've got to simply start digging.

As unbelievable as it seems, and though few will admit it, I believe there are people who will prefer to hold on to their low expectations of themselves rather than believe they are beings of the highest order. Some will choose to remain in the empty dungeon of poverty rather than experience the freedom of riches. Even domestic animals will settle for remaining in the comfortable surroundings of a cage rather than take on the responsibility of finding their own food. And there are also those who will hold fast to their history of having a bad attitude rather than let others know they have a heart of flesh and not a heart of stone.

They would rather do it because it requires neither effort nor a commitment to change. The self-destructing desire to stay 'comfortable' outweighs the desire to become uncomfortable. Getting out of our comfort zone is never a cinch and it's never comfortable.

In order to save yourself from the prison walls of comfort; make the art of leaning on someone else totally unnecessary. Of course it's O.K. to ask for help, but to give others power over your life or expect them to sustain your life with goods and services is immoral.

www.sparkplug.net

SPARK PLUG
POINTS TO PONDER

1. It's rather difficult to like someone else if you do not like yourself.

2. Because our vision is so limited, we never know how the story of our life will end.

3. If we faithfully picked up the pieces of our dream from where we are, we can still complete our mission.

4. I think most of us live our lives in silent frustration because we are too busy comparing our lives to others.

5. Change is difficult because we make it so.

"They were bright stars for a moment, and then they faded."

- Sam Walton

Chapter 3

Spark Plug Attitude!
Wherefore Art Thou?

Aspark plug attitude is definitely a valuable possession. It is the topic of discussion in homes, schools, board rooms, conference rooms, locker rooms, organizations and meeting rooms all over this country. Spark plug attitudes are being requested in job descriptions and barren relationships are hungry for its gusto. We're delighted to be around others who have a great attitude or positive outlook on life.

Those who seek to have a spark plug attitude are clearly the benefactors of our society. They are the mentors, motivators, and good corporate citizens who seek not fanfare but inner fulfillment through their positive contributions. They are the ones who continue to make this world a better place for our children and grandchildren.

Spark Plug Attitude: The Only Way to Fly

A Harvard University research study has found that attitude is the first cousin of achievement. This interesting study proved that 85% of the people that get hired or promoted on their jobs is directly related to their attitudes. Furthermore, a university research program was set up to find the components in the formula for success. They concluded that the required factors were *I.Q. knowledge, skills and attitude.*

After this fascinating research was completed, it was reported that attitude accounted for an astonishing 93% of success! Think about that for a second; a whopping 93% of your success can be attributed to your attitude.

Of all the sales organizations I've had the pleasure of working with, the sales manager always revealed that the top performers were the people with lot's of energy and enthusiasm.

Bad Attitudes
Drive People Away

At the other end of the spectrum, a Human Relations training firm identified the top ten business conduct mistakes that often drive people away. Number one on the list was bad attitudes. No one wants to do business, befriend or be served by people with a poor disposition.

Usually, these tormented souls don't like their job, where they live, or the people around them. They have a derogatory name for those they come in contact with and *seldom* honor their word. Constantly, they inject a lethal dose of doom and gloom into the lives of their family, neighbors and co-workers. They also believe they are inferior. By the same token, they tend to label everyone else as incompetent and untrustworthy. Consequently, they will never reach their potential because of their belief that someone else is holding them back.

These debilitating ways of thinking can blot out your career, negatively affect your health, alienate your friends and even rob you of your own life. Your ability to be creative, your unique skills, persistence, faith and a spark plug attitude can determine whether you rise to the top of the heap or dwell among the lackluster crowd of mediocrity. No one ever suggested that reaching your goals would be a soft bed of ease but a spark plug attitude can provide some shock absorbers for the ride.

The late Earl Nightingale summed it up best when he concluded that "A poor attitude equals poor results, a good attitude equals good results and a great attitude equals great results."

We have the power to *choose* our attitudes in every situation. It's a God-given power. If you are letting other people or dismal circumstances decide what kind of attitude you're going to have, you're giving your power away. I don't believe anyone wants to intentionally give their power away.

When the Facts Are Not the Truth

Yes, we simply have an attitude about absolutely everything.

At the height of the cola wars, *Pepsi* beat Coca Cola taste tests all around the country. The results maintained that Pepsi won the battle hands down, and was voted the best tasting soft drink. However, the *truth* of the matter was when it was time to buy a cola, people purchased Coca Cola 2 to 1 over Pepsi. Why? Because they had a better attitude about Coke.

People remember ordering a Coke on their first date. We all

remember seeing Coca Cola around the house when we were growing up and we really believed it when Coke affirmed it was the "real thing." Coca Cola is familiar to us, we are comfortable with it and we trust its name. Our *attitude* about Coke was one of the factors that established brand loyalty.

Life is all about *attitude!* It is not restricted to the traditions of the *past* because if life was solely based on the past, Heather Whitestone would not have been the first deaf Miss America in 1995. It took her six long years to learn how to say her last name. The reporters wanted to know how she was able to overcome such insurmountable odds. Heather gracefully replied, "My mother always told me when I was a little girl that the last four letters of American spell *I CAN.*"

Life is about attitude! It is not about your shortcomings. Life is about turning your dreary days into sunshine and enduring the pain that is thrust into your path. You've got to remember that the sun is always shining somewhere in this world and sooner or later it will shine on you. It's about attitude!

If life was about *facts,* Muggsy Bogues would not be 5'3" playing in the NBA. He's been playing professional basketball for eleven straight years in the land of the giants where the average height is 6'6" tall. Muggy's full height only reaches the waist of Michael Jordan!

Life is not entirely about your education. More than 20 years after Tom E. Dupree, Jr. flunked twice out of Georgia Tech, he bounced back and became a hero for that same prestigious school. His gift of $20 million dollars has been recorded as the largest endowment ever given to a U.S. business college by an individual. Dupree's name is on the School of Management at Georgia Tech.

Here's another fact that wasn't the truth. John Hastie, a former aerospace engineer discovered that a *razor blade doesn't dull* but slightly bends and becomes distorted each time it is used. He developed a magnetic gadget called the *Razor Mate* which actually realigns the blade back to its original shape. So the result of what you get is a 'new blade' with an increased shelf life of about 10 times longer.

As we become older, we lose our ability to think like a beginner. Most people have been programmed to just accept whatever they hear as the truth. They really don't want to rock the boat by asking questions. Dr. Robert Kriegle's book, *If It Ain't Broke, Break It* will definitely send you for a tailspin if you are a straight-laced business professional. His philosophy will utterly amaze you. It has truly inspired me to become more creative and ask more questions about the "facts."

Pizzaz! The Stuff a Spark Plug Attitude Is Made of

Unfortunately, the masses let situations, circumstances and other people control their attitudes instead of being their own captain. People often quip, "Once I get that promotion, ideal job or get married, then my life will change and my attitude will change for the better." Well, it never works that way. You will need a spark plug attitude in the beginning because it's steam for your engine. It actually takes you where you want to go.

Whatever you want to do, most often than not, your attitude will determine your destiny. The wrong attitude or a defeatist mentality toward a particular task will not give you the necessary momentum to do the best possible job. Even having the wrong attitude toward people who are different can cause you to miss rich blessings and golden opportunities. But with the right attitude, you have a first class ticket to wherever you want to go.

Start smiling more often. It's therapy for your face. As a matter of fact break out in a serious laugh every now and then. If people want to conclude that you are out of your mind, don't worry. Is anyone really normal or better yet . . . what is normal?

"Is Annette working today?"

(The inquisitive lady who was patiently standing at the customer service counter hardly resembled a relative or a long lost friend.)

"No, she'll be in tomorrow" the clerk solemnly replied.

"What about Yvette, is she here?"

"No, Yvette is not here either. Ma'am, can I help you with something?" the clerk asked.

(The lady seemed to ignore the question.)

"Well, can I have their schedule?" the lady grumbled.

"OK . . . Monday; 2-close, Wednesday; 10-3. Thursday 12-6, Friday . . . " she began to hastily record Annette and Yvette's schedule.

"Thank you, I'll just come back when they are here."

I couldn't begin to count the number of times this little scene occurred in the Captain D's where I was a manager many years ago. I had never seen anyone refuse to eat because their favorite people were not on duty. But Annette and her twin sister Yvette didn't just concentrate on selling fish, chips and a glass of tea with a lemon twist. As Jeff Blackman, the author of *Peak Your Profits* noted, they 'raised the ceiling' of the quality of customer service in a fast food restaurant.

Never did I hear them use the monotone . . . "Can I take your order *p-l-e-a-s-e* or the robotic, "Can -- I-- help -- you?" They were actually *happy* to serve the customers.

What was it about Annette and Yvette?

They knew how to make people feel special. Their very presence in the restaurant was more important to the customers than the fish and chips they served. It was not some phony act.

Who says you can't have customers asking for you by name at a fast food restaurant or any other business? With the right attitude, you can be a celebrity regardless of where you work.

What are you doing to rise above the crowd?

In our quest to become a technological giant, we've lost the "personal touch." It happens to be our most important piece of salesmanship and will remain a precious commodity. I really don't believe people are impressed with patronizing businesses that herd them around like cattle.

Arthur Loften, my old Navy comrade, amazed me with his uncanny ability to quickly befriend anyone. He is by far one of the most gifted and amusing storytellers I have ever heard. Loften sometimes kept the whole crew awake until 2:00 a.m., spellbound by his stories.

We would hang on his every word while he eloquently shared comical, animated, and compelling tales about his Navy adventures. Everyone knew Big Loft. He had friends at every port.

When he went away on duty at other ports, the entire department was lifeless. On occasion, Loften called in to say "hello." We all huddled around the phone in hopes of catching some sparks from his enthusiasm. The staff actually waited in line (single file) to talk to him. We treated him as if he was the highest ranking official in the Navy. He gave us respect and made us feel important. He got the same honor. In our eyes, Lofton was a *huge* celebrity.

What do your fair-weather friends or co-workers say when they see you coming? Do they greet you with a wide grin or turn to flee in another direction? What signals are you sending to other people? When you don't show up for work, would you say your department is *'just not the same'* or are they *throwing a big party and dancing to the beat?*

SPARK PLUG
POINTS TO PONDER

1. A Harvard University study proved that 85% of the people that get hired or promoted on their jobs is directly related to their attitudes.

2. History has proven that a spark plug attitude is more important than expertise.

3. If you have a spark plug attitude, there are no limits to your success.

4. With the right attitude, you can be a celebrity regardless of where you work.

5. The best thing about attitude is that we have the *power to choose* our attitudes in every situation.

"Whatsoever thy hand findeth to do, do it with thy might; for there is no work, nor device, nor knowledge, nor wisdom, in the grave, whither thou goest."

- Ecclesiastes 9:10

Chapter 4

Commitment:

A Seed That Yields Abundant Fruit

Webster defines commitment as a pledge or promise to do something. I like the candid definition that says *"Keep your word even when you change your mind."*

It's easy to keep our word when we're excited about something that we found rather interesting. But what about when our enthusiasm loses its spark?

Do you fulfill the words that you have sent forth into the universe or do you decide to abandon the ship just because you changed your mind? On occasion, we are all guilty of this error. But remember, that there is a reward in your faithfulness. You will never know the positive impact you are making on your life and the lives of others by keeping promises and commitments.

Commitment Holds Things Together

The desire to make a pledge or promise to do something requires responsibility or accountability. You won't find too many people who are willing to take responsibility for their actions. These same people usually lack a commitment to their goals and do not strive for excellence. Frantically, they are always in search of a loop hole and tend to *give up* when the pressures of life feel like a cement brick dangling around their necks. Sadly, all of their work seems to lie in an *unfinished* heap.

Imagine what our world would consist of if everyone refused to commit themselves to what they do. The quality of the building in which we work would be so poor it would probably collapse. The clothing we wear would be discarded after one good use because of poor production. The car we drive would have to be taken to the repair shop daily. Business deals would seldom be made and sales would rarely take place.

Commitment is not always an easy task. It will sometimes require us to press our way to engagements we no longer feel like attending. We often have to deal with people in which we would rather have no dealings at all. Even though a lack of commitment abounds in society, you can still be a person of your WORD.

If you find that you are making commitments to others that you have no intentions of keeping -- save everyone some trouble by not committing.

Providence Demands Commitment

Commitment will bring rewards to us that are greater than we can imagine. I don't believe in pure luck when it comes to achieving goals and making dreams come true. I don't believe there are any lucky people. However, there are millions of people in the world waiting for luck to come knocking at their door.

Millions are also deceived because they are looking for lady luck in the lottery. She flashes her brilliant smile of untold treasures, plays the song of the siren and weaves a web made only for those who are looking for a quick fix. Many die without putting forth an effort to achieve their goals and their feeble attempt to live an abundant life turns to ashes.

Sure, there are times when people receive things they didn't really earn or stumble upon opportunities without seeking them. But 'luck' is one of those words or ideas that often lures others into a false world of "expectancy without effort."

The most unfortunate person is the one who came to this earth, grew old, and left without leaving a trace. They never took the time to positively nourish someone else's life or stand up for their dreams. It was the distinguished Horace Mann who trumpeted, "Be ashamed to die unless you have won some victory for humanity." What are you doing to leave the world a little better than you found it?

Total commitment is planting a seed or idea, nurturing it, and being steadfast until your goal or dream is achieved. It means faithfully weathering the hardships of life because you know brighter days are ahead. I think the often quoted Goethe and W. H. Murray summed it up best when they stated. . .

Until one is committed there is hesitancy, the chance to draw back, always ineffectiveness. Concerning all acts of initiative (and creation) there is one elementary truth, the ignorance of which kills countless ideas and splendid plans:

that the moment one definitely commits oneself, then Providence moves too. All sorts of things occur to help one that would never otherwise have occurred. A whole stream of events issues from the decision, raising in one's favor all manner of unforeseen incidents and meetings and material assistance, which no man could have dreamed would have come his way.

Whatever you can do, or dream you can, begin it. Boldness has genius, power and magic in it.

Providence does not begin to move until you begin to move. From the very moment commitment is manifested in your life, you can begin to look forward to small miracles that inspire you to keep moving toward your goal.

Nothing Stands In the Way of Commitment!

In the summer of '93, I started my business in advertising and publishing. All of my efforts were centered around providing affordable advertising to small business owners on a community basis. But just when I was halfway finished with my second directory, I was involved in a near fatal car accident.

I crashed into a stalled car at top speed on Hwy. 285 in Atlanta, Georgia while someone else smashed my car in the rear! If I was ever going to have a test that would measure my commitment, this would probably be the one. It is only in the fires of life that we have an opportunity to get an assessment of our dedication to our work, family, goals, etc.

My car was a total loss. It was crushed as if it was a thin piece of aluminum foil. The driver side door had to be ripped from its hinges. I was stuck behind the wheel like a sumo wrestler pinned to the canvas.

After I was skillfully removed from the car, I was immediately rushed to the hospital.

Thankfully . . . they discharged me on the same day. I suffered a slight cut on the top of my head, a lacerated lip and severe internal pain. After getting home, I realized the accident had made headline news on television that evening. It was a miracle that I survived!

During that time I was a one-man show, operating my business on a tight budget. All of my funds had gone into starting the business. It never occurred to me that everything would literally come to a screeching halt.

I was completely helpless for three long weeks. I had no income and of course there were debts that needed to be paid. I had no transportation, no relatives in town and my insurance company was refusing to pay for damages. But I was still committed to getting my publication out at any cost.

While I was lying in excruciating pain for those three weeks, I didn't focus on having a pessimistic attitude. I didn't wallow in self pity and ask "God why did you let this happen to me?" I was optimistic.

I asked questions like, "How can I get out of this situation and turn this whole thing around? How can I overcome this calamity?" Since I was still alive, I had just enough faith to believe that everything would work out for the good regardless of the state of my physical condition.

My brother came up from Savannah to visit me and offered to lend me some cash. After paying some huge bills, my account was literally running on empty. I had a big decision to make-- either pay my rent or put the money down on a car. Well, I decided to put the money down on a car and work hard the next week.

That following Monday, I made three big sales on my first day back to work. I was determined to honor my word that I had given out to my clients. Two months later, I successfully completed and distributed my second publication because I was committed to my goal and my prayers were answered.

Get Serious!

A lack of commitment has terminated promising jobs, destroyed families, broken marriages, alienated children, ravaged communities, ruined relationships, devalued society and the list can go on and on. But if you want to make a name for yourself, let it be one that people can look to and say there stands someone who is committed to what they do.

A great philosopher once stated that "One single pursuit is the easiest road to success." Putting your heart and soul into one single idea really makes a difference. Being totally dedicated to one idea can actually help you accomplish a great deal and provide more substance, depth and creativity to your work. Whatever you decide to do, be 100% committed.

Commitment is the key ingredient that is 'lacking in so many and gifted to a few' (a quote I picked up from one of my friends). We should instill the real value of commitment in our children. Either we aren't setting good examples or they consistently ignore our words. We now have a generation of people who don't or won't commit to anything.

Let Passion Be Your Pilot

Quick. What are you passionate about? You would do it for free. It is as natural as breathing.

Did you come up with anything? When it comes to your life's work, it is very important that you find something that you *really* love to do and commit to it with all of your heart.

Of course, every line of work has its share of "little things you would rather not have to do." But I've learned that when you're involved in something you are passionate about, life takes on a whole new meaning. It's easier to commit and your reward is complete inner fulfillment.

You have found your passion when you begin to do the things that Berton Braley talks about in this often quoted poem.

If you want a thing bad enough to go out and fight for it,
To work day and night for it,
To give up your time, peace and sleep for it,
If all you dream and scheme are about it,
And life seems useless and worthless without it.
If you'd gladly sweat for it, and fret for it
And lose all of your terror of the opposition for it.
If you simply go after the thing that you want
With all of your capacity, strength and sagacity,

Faith, hope and confidence and stern pertinacity,
If neither cold, poverty, famine, nor gout,
Sickness nor pain, of body and brain
Can keep you from the thing that you want,
If dogged and grim you beseech and beset it
With the help of GOD you will surely get it!

Are you willing to do whatever it takes (legally and morally) to keep your commitment? Will sickness, pain, apathy or a broken heart prevent you from reaching your goal? Will fear sink its teeth deeply into your soul and leave you confused, doubtful and immobilized? When the going gets tough, will you decide to cancel everything and live a life of *could have been*? Will family members and associates persuade you to give up on your dream?

I challenge you today to hold firm to your commitment and see it through until the end. Plant your dreams in a garden of belief and let your passion guide you toward your purpose!

Do Your Best & Move on!

I remember what I thought was the most horrible speaking engagement of my life. I had decided to do my very first seminar on *Overcoming Your Fears.*

My fiancee at the time, who is now my wife told me not to try to memorize the speech word-for-word because I might get on stage and forget what I was supposed to say. Well, like most men, I did not listen.

I quickly replied, "I can do it. I'll do just fine."

She simply said, "OK."

On the evening of the seminar after my award winning introduction, I dashed onto the stage. I was ready to dazzle the audience with my power-packed presentation. Suddenly, my mind went on vacation without my approval and all I could see were bright lights shining in my face. Beyond the blinding lights was only a sea of darkness. I couldn't see anything or anyone. I couldn't even remember my name, let alone my speech that I thought I had carefully folded and tucked away in my mind.

I moaned to myself, "Surely this couldn't be happening to me, I know this speech like the back of my hand!"

Everything was a blur. Sweat was rolling down my forehead like raindrops on a windshield. My heart was literally beating like the hooves of horses on hot dry pavement. (Thumpety, thumpety, thump.) Embarrassment was flowing out of my soul like a mighty stream. I tried looking around to find Jacqueline in the audience to somehow get a glimpse of someone familiar or maybe uncover a shred of hope by seeing her face but the lights were too bright on the stage. I tried to present my speech just as I had done countless times before, at home, in the car, in the checkout line, etc. It would not come forth! My mouth was dry and I desperately wanted to *crawl* off the platform and *run* for cover.

The wrath of dead silence in the huge auditorium was tormenting me and I could feel a multitude of glistening eyes glaring at me through the darkness.

I was considering the idea of obeying the thundering voice in my head that bellowed "Get off the stage, just walk off . . . you're making a complete fool of yourself . . . who do you think you are anyway?!" when ever so slowly, the information began to filter my mind so that I could make sense to my audience.

Evidently I must have done a really good job.

After the speech, people came up thanked me for what they thought was an outstanding presentation. Surprisingly, a lady called me up a year and a half later to get what she described as 'very useful' information.

I guess it was one of those times when God has mercy on us and plays an award winning symphony around whatever we do from the heart!

Get Back in And Try Again

Jacqueline and I both knew that my presentation was missing a "spark." As a matter of fact, when I was practicing, I could have won an award for *Mr. Speaker* of the year. But after that lukewarm speech, I had big knot in my stomach. I told myself that all the other professional speakers could have the speaking business to themselves. I didn't want to stand up on a lonely stage ever again or stare into a sea of darkness for the rest of my life. Yet, deep in my heart, I knew I had a message to share with others that was bubbling over and it could not be contained. Life would not let me rest until I recommitted myself to becoming a professional inspirational/motivational speaker.

One week later, my friend Lisa Jones extended an invitation for me to give the keynote address to 850 students at Camp Creek Middle School in College Park, Georgia. It was the largest group I had ever spoken to at one time. I was able to redeem myself. I had learned my lesson the hard way. Memorizing a speech word-for-word would always be number one on my speaker's list of "thou shalt nots." It may *work* for others, but not for me.

Early in my speaking career I was also hesitant about joining Toastmasters. I didn't think I had enough skills to be a part of the organization. I just knew I wasn't good enough. But if I was going to be committed to public speaking, I had to master the basics. I also had to apply the principle of feeling the fear and doing it anyway as Dr. Susan Jeffers says in her book of the same name, *Feel the Fear and Do It Anyway*.

After joining Toastmasters, I found that it was one of the most warm and friendliest environments for anyone who wanted to become more at ease when speaking in public. I went on to speak at more than 50 clubs around the city and became one of the most sought after speakers in the organization. Once again, it was my commitment that made the difference.

Since that humbling experience on stage, I have started *Spark Plug International*, a professional speaking and training business. I've continued to inspire thousands of people in corporations, and organizations around the country because of my commitment to make a difference.

How many tasks have you started only to put aside after you became frustrated? *Repetition* is the foundation of success. Commitment is *necessary*. Falling on your face is *required*. Determination is *essential*.

What if you decided you would give up on learning how to walk when you were a child? (Falling down was just too embarrassing. Or you refused to continue to *humiliate* yourself by falling down.) Would you be walking today?

If you are trying to complete a worthy task without a strong commitment, it's almost like trying to eat soup with a toothpick or getting a giraffe climb a tree. So go back and get that idea, take that class, pull out that puzzle or whatever it was you laid aside. Dust it off and give it another try.

You and I know that until you have given it all you've got, you cannot honestly say you've *really* tried. You will always wonder if you would have succeeded had you stuck it out. Don't spend your whole life wondering, get busy. The world is waiting for you to do it.

Whatever you would like to do, wherever you would like to go, or whatever you would like to become, be committed. Your commitment will make the difference.

Make a commitment to yourself that you will be known for something that you literally pour your heart into, i.e., speaker, teacher, writer, entrepreneur, manager, scientist, musician, banker, carpenter, plumber, tennis player, computer guru, etc. Become known for having a commitment to excellence in all that you do.

Mothers and fathers, please continue to instill the importance of commitment in your children. This can make the difference between a committed citizen and an apathetic citizen.

SPARK PLUG
POINTS TO PONDER

1. The world would *really* be a dismal place if no one committed to anything.

2. Whatever you decide to do, be 100% committed.

3. Providence does not begin to move until you begin to move.

4. Success is planting a seed or idea, nourishing it and being committed to it until your goal or dream is achieved.

5. Commitment is not an easy task, it sometimes requires us to press our way to engagements we no longer 'feel' like attending.

I'm going to be happy today!

Though the skies are cloudy and gray

No matter what comes my way

I'm going to be happy today!

- Ella Wheeler Wilcox

Chapter 5

Attitude of Fortitude

Let's face it! Most of us who have tried to do anything worthwhile realize the 'gates of hell' swing wide open when we finally make up our minds to follow our dream. All kinds of gruesome pests come out of the woodwork. They try to irritate us and hinder our efforts to move forward. We often wonder if we made the *right* decision to *step out* of our comfort zone.

One thing is for certain, you'll always find that an 'uphill battle' is usually on the menu of "things worth doing." But persistence, an attitude of fortitude, or the will to stay in the race is a sure ticket to progress.

Massive achievement has never been without the company of persistence. Having the attitude to get up no matter how many times you fall is essential. As the ancient proverb eloquently states, "If you're knocked down seven times, get up eight."

The airplane was not a huge success on the very first attempt. The clock was not completed on the first attempt; neither was the television, fax, telephone, computer, Sega CD nor Web TV successfully completed on the first try.

Nothing great was ever achieved on the first endeavor. Trial and error are as normal as the sun shining each day. But we have the notion that we must succeed the first time we try anything. The results you want will often take more than a few attempts.

It's O.K. To Fumble

"You made a mistake. Shame on you!" society screams.

Mistakes are taboo, a no-no. They are the embarrassing acts which cause us to shy away from the things we really want in life. But the rare souls who understand the process of doing anything worthwhile realize that mistakes can produce massive success. As a matter of fact, business managers have been known to encourage their people to make mistakes on a regular basis. The employees actually learn more. Eventually, they make more contributions to the organization than those who are afraid to take risks. So hang in there!

I like what Calvin Coolidge proclaimed about persistence:

Nothing takes the place of persistence,
Talent will not,
The world is full of unsuccessful people with talent.
Education will not,
The world is full of educated derelicts.
Genius will not,
Unrewarded genius is almost a proverb.
Persistence and determination alone are omnipotent.

A lack of persistence can cause you to miss your calling and forfeit everything you've longed to be. There are many who have marvelous ideas but they are not persistent about moving the idea from the intangible to the tangible. Unless there is a willingness to keep pushing, your 'good ideas' will never come into fruition. The idea gets stuck somewhere between your excitement and taking action. Are you still sitting on your great idea?

When it comes to your ideas, guard them well. Beware of the faithless few. They're usually the ones you thought would cheer you onward. They are the ones who will ask where you got that 'crazy' idea and label you as a crackpot. They will hang around just to sprinkle doubt on your ideas and enthusiasm. More often than not, it is their own fear speaking on their behalf. They are afraid; therefore, they will try to cast their fear upon you.

When I attended the 1997 National Speakers Convention in Anaheim, California, Lou Holtz, the former football coach of Notre Dame blared, "The only people that will tell you it cannot be done are the people who have *never* accomplished anything!"

Even though you may be caught up in your own excitement about your dreams, it is not good to share them with everyone. Treat your ideas and dreams as something sacred because they are. Find people who will support you or operate solely on your inner strength.

Sylvester Stallone understood the power of persistence. In high school, he was voted most likely to end up in the electric chair. He was even homeless at one time -- sleeping in a bus terminal with other homeless people. After receiving numerous rejections from Hollywood producers for his first film, *Rocky*, he never gave up. He was told on many occasions that the movie was corny and it would never be a box office success.

Yet, *Rocky* delighted fans all over the world and received an Academy Award for best picture of the year after its release.

Peter J. Daniels failed every single grade in school and now has successful companies all around the globe. He didn't learn to read until he was about 25 years old. His teacher Mrs. Phillips, told him that he would never amount to anything. He has now written a book as a *lesson* to his teacher entitled, *Mrs. Phillips, You Were Wrong.*

I urge you to read biographies of people who succeeded in spite of the obstacles they faced. You will definitely be ignited with inspiration to continue your journey. Reading about the lives of others is a testimony that offers encouragement for your own life.

Persist Until Something Happens

What do great people have in common? They all persisted against the odds. They developed a dogged determination to stay in the race no matter what happened. They kept their eyes focused on their goals and were not distracted by the feeble opinions of others. They made a decision, a firm commitment and kept chipping away at the mountain until it became a pebble.

I was very persistent about getting started in the public speaking business. I gave multitudes of complimentary speeches to get my foot in the door to any group who would listen and became a member of various groups such as Toastmasters International, Georgia Speakers Association, and National Speakers Association. I literally consumed every book I could get my hands on about the fundamentals of public speaking.

I stayed up late many nights developing and practicing my presentation and attended countless seminars. I constantly asked questions of those who were already in the business. On occasion, my wife had to wake me up around 2:00 a.m. and prod me up the stairs to the comfort of the bed.

Once she woke me up past midnight and was stunned to see that though I was sound asleep, the pen that was clutched in my hand was still in the writing position, touching the paper. (I guess I fell asleep in the middle of a thought.) I was totally unyielding in my determination to learn the business. I was willing to do whatever was necessary because I found something I loved to do and I wanted to do it with my whole heart!

I don't burn the midnight oil as much as I did in the early years but I still work on my craft every single day.

Read extensively about any topic that interests you. Go to seminars and workshops to learn more and meet other people who are like minded. I have discovered that if you want anything bad enough and you are willing to persist, it will happen for you.

What Are You Persistently Doing?

A merry-go-round can persistently go round and round and still not go anywhere! We all persist at something whether it's productive or not so productive. Some people persistently go to jobs they don't like and never make an effort to figure out what they would *enjoy* doing. They remain in unfruitful relationships that are sometimes life threatening, they watch everything on television that causes the soul to become malnourished and listen to too much racket on the radio.

On the other hand, there are some who spend quality time elevating their thinking, expanding their possibilities and exercising their creativity. They enjoy the fresh beauty of nature, read inspirational books, and take the time to make a difference in their communities. They listen to inspiring tapes or CDs, exercise, talk to loved ones about hopes and dreams, and limit the amount of T.V. they watch to a few hours per week. You already possess this power of persistence, sometimes you just have to redirect it.

The people who succeed in life and do great things are still ordinary people who do extraordinary things. If you look at the big picture, they had a goal they wanted to accomplish and decided they would do something that Og Mandino says so beautifully in his book *The Greatest Salesman in the World*, "I will persist until I succeed."

Another important aspect of having an attitude of fortitude is knowing when to change directions. You've got to know when to create another plan to accomplish the same goal. Staying on course sometimes means making a right or left turn. But don't fret; as long as the needle of your compass is still pointing toward your dream, you can find your way.

Struggling Through the Tunnel

Interestingly enough, I saw the movie *Jerry McGuire* and it reminded me of the tunnel of life that we often experience. Jerry, who was the main character, had a very difficult time finding himself or making it through the tunnel, but eventually he made it through. We must enter this same tunnel at various intervals in our life if we are to become wiser human beings.

Everyone gets a taste of what I'd like to mildly refer to as the 'tunnel' of life. It's a time when everything seems to be shaken from its foundation. It's a time in our human existence when we lose *someone* we deeply care about (best friend, mother, father, husband, wife, child, girlfriend, boyfriend, etc.) through death or a terminated relationship. The loss could also be character, dignity, a job, money, home, a car, an heirloom, etc.

Sometimes the temperature in the tunnel is bitter cold, at other times the sweltering heat is unbearable. There is no candle to hold as you are literally jerked and pulled through this lifeless place of despair. The sun does not shine and there are no flowers or any other kinds of plant life in the tunnel.

Take note. I did not say there is no light because there are some places that will shed divine light on areas of your life.

While in this tunnel, you really don't know how long it will be before you can see your way again. On your lonely journey you discover how merciless the world has really become. You discover who your true friends are or if you have any at all.

It is really a time of 'sifting' or dealing with issues that have been overlooked until your journey led you into the tunnel. It is a time of letting go and exercising forgiveness. Life has a way of forcing us to come to a place where we experience this overdue inner cleansing.

The tunnel has a cornucopia of blessings to offer if we are willing to fight the dragons that lurk inside. That's right, *fight* the dragons. The only way you are going to get your blessing is to fight for it! However, you just might experience a multitude of sleepless nights, poor eating habits, loneliness, hopelessness or lose a few friends in the process.

The tunnel is designed to be a place of pain and unrest because the surroundings are fertile for giving birth to strong character, wisdom, sensitivity and forgiveness. It is an effective way to learn the lessons you need for the rest of life's complex and intriguing journey.

If you are determined to successfully make it through the tunnel, you will undoubtedly find abundant life and healing on the other side. If you can keep your mind and heart pure, then you have mastered the test. Hopefully you will become better rather than bitter. If you become a better person, you have earned the wisdom that is attached to the journey. You are ready for the next tunnel. You are now equipped to help someone else through the tunnel which you have just departed. You are also required to give them what you were not given, i.e., patience, time, love, understanding, mercy and forgiveness.

Unfortunately, the real tragedy is the number of people who have gotten stuck in the tunnel. They lost all hope of ever being delivered. They stopped fighting. The hunger for freedom was swallowed up in sorrow, criticism and depression. No one offered them a helping hand. There were no warm, friendly, sincere, smiling faces of encouragement.

I'm sure you can remember a few tunnels through which you have traveled. You will find them sparingly or generously sprinkled along the highway of life. I believe they are the stimuli for growth and development.

Every tunnel has its own personality. But if you can remember to take your *spark plug attitude* with you, it will definitely help you discover your unique and precious gems of wisdom a lot sooner. Real appreciation of the journey can only be seen from the top of the mountain or from the completion of the experience. The weary days and worrisome nights, the times when you just knew you couldn't take one more step, will all come together to form a clearer, brighter picture.

No matter who you are, where you live, or how beautiful, talented, educated and powerful you are, hardships will come. Whether it involves finances, relationships, suffering, abandonment, or death in the family, it will find you. It is not given to us to know how long we must endure our trials and tribulations. It is not given to us to know what trials lie ahead but whatever the trial may be, *it must pass!* Sometimes it may be hours, days, weeks, months or years before we receive an answer to our dilemma. But the answer will come. Every story has an ending. Nothing really lasts forever.

Fear will always creep inside and take advantage of the opportunity to coax us into a den of deception. It will try and persuade us to think we will never get to the end of the long and winding the tunnel. Time will slowly pass as if it's in no hurry to bring comfort or compassion. The waiting period can be very humiliating. Weariness will seep into our souls. Yet the most important thing is what we become during the process of our afflictions.

Think back *for a moment* (not *too* long) to the last time you had the opportunity to experience something that trampled mercilessly upon your heart. The pain was so great that you lost all sense of reasoning. You lost your appetite for food and everything else that promotes vitality. All the diamonds or gold in the world could not ease the pain. The people you cared about the most showed the least respect and showered the most criticism upon you.

It probably seemed as if you had lost your way forever and there was no one or nothing to guide you back onto the path of joy and happiness. You may have felt that you were the only person living on this planet drinking from the cold cup of suffering, or the only person walking in the valley of death. You wondered where God was while you were fighting for your life.

Eventually . . . you experienced deliverance. The sun began to brightly shine again and it slowly melted the cynical stone in your soul. You felt whole again. It was as if the insufferable event never took place. This is the circle of life that teaches patience and endurance. It is life's acid test that often comes to make and mold us, measure our durability and prepare us to experience true greatness.

It is likely that you could be in stormy waters right now but tomorrow you may be sailing in the sea of serenity. Without the violent storms there would be no sincere appreciation of the warm, bright and sunny days. Without having the opportunity to taste the bitter seed of hate, love wouldn't seem so precious.

SPARK PLUG
POINTS TO PONDER

1. Many people have great ideas but they are not persistent about having that great idea come into fruition.

2. Another important aspect of having an attitude of fortitude is knowing when to change directions.

3. Develop a dogged determination to stay in the race no matter what happens.

4. Nothing great was ever achieved on the first try.

5. Trial and error are a natural part of life.

"If we are to confidently merge onto the highway of change, we must first rearrange our thinking."

- Jacqueline Thomas

Chapter 6

Thoughts: The Dictators Of Your Life

"Your thoughts will eventually shape your whole life." This bit of wisdom is as old as the hills but it carries a profound message. If you don't take your thoughts by the horns and control them, they will ultimately control you. They can either lead you to the brink of death or guide you toward vibrant health, peace, happiness and love. They can cause you to feel like a prince/princess in an opulent palace or a pauper behind prison walls. Iron bars are not always required to confine a prisoner.

Sometimes it is simply our own thoughts that create barriers to a better quality of life for ourselves and our family.

Are your thoughts helping you to give and do your very best? Conversely, are they tearing your inner nature to shreds? Have they stolen your dreams, vision or purpose? Did they destroy your self-worth? Are you constantly preoccupied with what other people think about you? Are you still entertaining self-defeating thoughts of yesteryear or even yesterday?

You did not reach your level of thinking and reacting overnight. It may take a little time, patience and prayer if you are willing to begin the exciting journey toward change. Even though the road may be lonely, the riches you obtain, both tangible and intangible, will always outweigh the discomfort.

Our thought life is the most difficult area of our lives to tame. If we could strive to constantly 'focus on the good' for ourselves and humanity, how drastically different everything else would seem. I am not suggesting that your thoughts have the power to single handedly *change* everything. But they are the wheels in your mind that can determine all of your actions, thereby creating a positive or negative reaction in the universe.

We think at the rate of approximately 1300 words per minute and speak at a rate of 150 - 200 words per minute. What other people say to us is far less important than what we say to ourselves. Imagine having 1300 negative words per minute pounding your mind throughout the day like an elephant on a trampoline. Is it any wonder that most people are impatient, irritable, or have poor attitudes?

Would you like a better quality of life? If so, the change begins with a positive thought life. As we have heard so often, the *real* battle ground is in our own mind. You cannot move forward if your mind is holding you hostage in the past.

The best way to change is to start with small steps. We all know that one step at a time is easier than three steps at a time. You are not expected to slay the giant in one single blow just as David slew Goliath. But if you continue to keep focusing on the good, you will begin to experience a surge of strength that will definitely push you forward.

Guilt & Shame: The Twin Blades

Guilt and shame are so closely related that you cannot have one without the other. These evil twins can be very destructive but at times they can also be indicative of a healthy conscience. The world is always in need of those who seek to exercise good values and morals because it holds this country together.

Just think for a moment about the people who run for

political office. The first tactic usually begins with combing their past to find out if they have some guilt and shame that could use a little exposure.

Once it is revealed, the party begins. The mission is to find out how far the competition can be goaded before they surrender. Some give up, others decide to stay in the heated race. Those who stay in the race often wonder if it's worth all the humiliation and scrutiny.

Candidly speaking, we get no joy from being represented by public officers who deliberately abandon values and morals.

Though people may sometimes change, the media knows that changing our attitude about them is difficult. Consequently, we are often permitted to repeatedly condemn and convict them as we peer through the media's magnifying glass.

If you are willing to allow your life to become naked before your fellow citizens, run for public office or become a big celebrity.

The truth of the matter is we have all experienced guilt and shame from an act which was small or great. We're all guilty. But we feel better when we can take the spotlight off ourselves for a moment and magnify someone else's life.

It is often too painful for us to examine our own lives. But sooner or later you will have to face yourself in the mirror and either be pleased or disgusted, happy or sad. We make that decision every day based on how we live our lives and treat other people. Remember, we all have a story that could be published by those whose journalistic integrity remains questionable.

Few are willing to admit that we are all sitting on the edge of confusion about some of the mysteries of life. No one has it all together. No one has it all figured out. It is not wise to look up to anyone as if they were a god who holds all the answers to our problems.

Instead of immortalizing someone, the most appropriate gift we can give them is respect. One of the worst things that can happen in the life of another is to be in hot pursuit of a hero. At the end of every pursuit is some degree of disappointment.

Most people believe if they wallow in guilt and shame long enough they will be redeemed. Not so. It is merely a red flag for you to change your behavior in one direction or another. You will never be rewarded with righteousness by wallowing in the pool of guilt and shame.

Forgiveness: The Walls Must Come Tumbling Down!

Our whole world suffers from a lack of forgiveness.

Generations upon generations carry a seed that is potent with anger, strife, jealousy and prejudice. The sea of forgiveness seems dry and barren. But the bloody, messy sea of unforgiveness is filled to the brim and running over.

Despite what others may say, I still believe in order to jumpstart your heart, put a pep in your step and add life to your years, forgiveness is necessary. It has been found to be the cure of the ages. Its electrical current can reach clear across the ocean. It won't cost you a nickel and it will give you freedom that you never dreamed possible.

In which sea has your mind chosen to swim? Forgiveness or unforgiveness?

If you want to enjoy the benefits of a spark plug attitude, it demands that you forgive on a daily basis. Healing demands that you forgive. If you want peace in your life, you must forgive. In order to shut and lock the door to a painful past, forgiveness is the key.

I believe forgiveness is awkward for most of us because it requires that we give, lay something down or cast it aside.

Anne Frank wrote in her diary, "Give of yourself, give as much as you can. And you can always give something, even if it is only kindness." (There is no gift too insignificant or too large that comes from the heart.)

Forgiveness can be a healing ointment that flows into our past as an antidote for any hurt or pain. If you allow it to perform its task, it will hasten the recovery of the deepest wound. You will immediately feel younger and your vision will once again have clarity. Your whole life will be less stressful.

Soon you will begin to love yourself again because you now have the freedom to do so. The excess baggage has been cast aside so that you can experience a bright new beginning.

The real problem doesn't lie in being unable to forgive but merely refusing to forgive. In order to pick up the armor of love, we must painfully lay down the burden of hate.

Forgiveness is simple, yet sometimes tough, but necessary.

You've Got to Release Them From the Rusty Nail

There is an unrelenting howl from the belly of the earth to become hardened, bitter, cold and intolerant. Many of us heed the call, others fight to ignore its monstrous wails. Nevertheless, the call is continuous. We may *feel* powerful when we refuse to forgive others but in reality it is a manifestation of weakness.

How long must you let your friends, acquaintances, and

family members dangle on the rusty nail of unforgiveness? How long will you use your ineffective efforts to keep them in shackles? Letting them off the rusty nail is not for them, it is for your own peace of mind, health, prosperity, and happiness as well as posterity. There are no benefits in unforgiveness. The only payoff you will receive is the inability to fully enjoy the gift of life, an additional 10 years added to your face, a heavy burden on your heart and phantom physical ailments.

In order to embrace the present, the past must forever remain in the past. Forgiveness begins when you are strong, noble and willing enough to let it all go. It is *indeed* an act of humility. If you are interested in destroying your future, let your mind dwell in the swamp of the past. Let your decisions and your actions have their roots firmly planted in the soil of yesterday. Make sure that all of your creative energy is directed toward revenge and you will *never* experience the freedom of forgiving.

Frankly, we don't always feel that forgiveness should be extended to those who have caused us sorrow. At times we toil with the act of forgiveness and it causes us much grief. But dealing with the pain is one of the seeds for growth and healing. You've got to *feel* the pain. If you ignore or deny it, you will remain in bondage and hinder yourself from experiencing strong, fruitful relationships.

Grieving is healthy. So go ahead and grieve . . . *grieve a little more . . . grieve some more if you need to . . . then move on.*

I took a giant step toward healing when I forgave my father (or *released him*) for not participating in my life. He wasn't around to help me adapt socially or give me tips on successful living. He never took me fishing, taught me to drive, or told me about the responsibilities of being a man. He never saw me compete at tennis meets and probably never knew I eventually became a great player. He wasn't there to give me helpful hints on shaving, dating, or any other simplicities of life that required wisdom. When I heard my friends rave about their relationships with their fathers, I lamented over the fact that I never saw mine. Why couldn't *I* have a dad at home? Why didn't he love me, my sister and brother enough to call to make sure we were even still alive?

Sure, I still think about him and feel the icy stab in my heart every now and again. But I had to come to a place in my life where I had to forgive him because it was interfering with my progress. I had to let him go. I had to take him off the rusty nail where I had left him hanging for so long. He was not excused for ignoring I existed as his son. But I forgave him for the years of pain and suffering his negligence had caused.

The people that you need to forgive may never change. They may never acknowledge how they have mistreated you or how they have blemished your character. You may never feel that your mother or your father truly loves you but it is still imperative that you release them from that rusty nail. For your own sake, for your own sanity, for your own future, let it go. Love yourself enough to do it! Begin to walk in the warm, promising light of today so you can fulfill your purpose.

Release Yourself Too!

Releasing yourself from hanging on the rusty nail means dealing with the residue that guilt and shame have left behind. It must be dealt with in order to experience recovery. It is not yours to keep. Even if someone places the burden upon your back, it is still not yours to keep. People from your past will constantly remind you of your mistakes and faults but you are the person who must put yourself on the altar of forgiveness and stay there. You must start with loving, forgiving, and respecting yourself before you can pass the torch of love, respect and forgiveness to someone else. As the ancient African proverb says, "If there are no enemies within, the enemies without can do you no harm." Again, wallowing in guilt and shame is not a highway to righteousness. God's gift of forgiveness continually flows from the mercy seat and is available to everyone.

Worry Whittles Your Life Away

Peter J. Daniels defined worry as *"Creating mental pictures of the things you do not want."* Even though worry can be unproductive for us, we spend the vast majority of our precious time swimming in it. I agree with Daniels because all day long we are creating movies in our mind. It is our own little secret place that is either filled with happiness or sadness. We are in control of the pictures we create.

Negative thoughts come to us more often than positive ones but we don't have to pull out a chair and ask them to "stay awhile." Poof! In an instant, they can be gone.

When we take the focus off ourselves, we tend to worry less. For example, it has been proven that the mind can only concentrate *intensely* on one thought at a time. If your concentration is geared toward helping someone else, there's no room to wallow in worry. Sure the thoughts will come, but try grabbing an affirmation and hold on or lose yourself in helping others.

So what's it going to be? In the movie, *Shaw Shank*

Redemption, Morgan Freeman reminded us that we can either "Get busy living, or get busy dying."

My Cash Flow Is on Vacation

I would venture to say that 80% of all worry is related to insufficient finances. Money is the powerful driving force behind practically everything this world has to offer. There are people who earn millions of dollars every year, yet they die spiritually and financially destitute. They never became disciplined in their spending.

In our society, when you really evaluate the situation, your money matters are about the only thing you *can* control especially when you receive a weekly or monthly paycheck. You can save money no matter how meager you think your income may be. It merely requires consistency and starting immediately!

We are not fully in control of some sicknesses and diseases that come upon us. We cannot control the feelings that others have toward us. We certainly cannot control the weather. But we *can* control how much money we put aside for our future.

Thinking enough of yourself to pay yourself is sometimes difficult to do. Denying the wizardry of the media is not always easy to accomplish. The colorful ads beckon to us, the carefully selected music draws us into the picture and before we realize what is happening, we have fallen into the marketing trap. Gadgets for the kitchen, 'how to' books, the latest fashions, electronic toys, a vacation in Maui, anything that appeals to our ego helps to bury us in debt.

Most people get so caught up in the rat race that they make no plans for their financial future and wander into retirement with no clue as to how they will support themselves.

If you haven't started working on your financial future, go to the library *today* to find out how you can make your money grow or find a good broker. Few people know that $30 or $40 a month can purchase stocks in major corporations and a mere $50 can purchase savings bonds.

Increase your ability to earn more by taking classes, starting a business, cross training on the job or volunteering for more responsibility. How far you really go in this life is up to you. Learning a new language, traveling around the world or building a city, the ball's in your court.

www.sparkplug.net

SPARK PLUG
POINTS TO PONDER

1. If you do not monitor your thoughts and control them, they will ultimately control you.

2. Peter J. Daniels defines worry as "Creating mental pictures of things you do not want."

3. You are not expected to slay the giant in one single blow just as David killed Goliath.

4. It's OK to release *yourself* from the 'rusty nail' of unforgiveness.

5. In order to pick up the armor of love, we have to painfully lay down the burden of hate.

"We cannot become what we need to be by remaining what we are."

- Max De Pree

Chapter 7

Who's in Your Club?

It doesn't matter how much you read positive material or attempt to apply spiritual principles if you do not have character. My good friend Cecil Morris pointed this out to me once. It was something I never really took the time to think about but I found it to be quite true.

We live in an era where people are attempting to be 'spiritual' but often have no semblance of the *fruit* that resembles a life of spirituality.

Spirituality is more than a state of mind. It's more than words that are spoken or scriptures that are quoted. It's more than a fad. It's more than a feeling. Actions tell the whole story.

When the essential element of character is missing, it leaves a gaping hole in everything you do. Most people will even be able to sense the inconsistency in you. They can clearly see that you are not who you claim to be.

The moral fiber of this nation has been stretched thinner than fiber optic cable. It's no wonder that many have just given up on humanity. If someone makes me a promise and I transfer the promise to someone else, my ability to keep that promise relies heavily on the first person who made it. If my hands are literally tied, their failure to keep their word usually prevents me from keeping mine. In other words, if they don't do what they said they would do, then I can't always do what I need to do. It is as simple as that. It's important to keep your word even if you change your mind. And yes, of course, I know . . . some things will always be out of our control.

I Want a Winning Team!

If you're my age, you might have to travel a little further, but travel back with me to junior high or high school. Do you remember your physical education class? When it was time to choose team members for softball, baseball, volleyball, kickball or soccer, you only wanted those who would help you win.

Right?

Well, what happened to the desire to make wise choices when it comes to winning in life? People, especially our young people, have a tendency to embrace the pessimistic mannerisms and attitudes of their comrades like water absorbed into a sponge. If you want to remain focused on fulfilling your purpose, you must constantly monitor the company you keep.

My job would be very burdensome if my wife vehemently denounced everything I did or criticized all of my suggestions for the business. On the other hand, her job would be difficult if I did likewise. We couldn't possibly make any real progress if we were weighing each other down with negativity. (We're usually able to agree on an idea and act on it immediately. It really makes the journey easier and the load much lighter when there's a little support.)

In general people are either doing one of two things. They are either sending you to the moon on a rocket or digging an early grave for you. Their words and actions are either pushing you forward with encouragement or pulling you back with negativity. I'm sure you will agree that you can do without those who are determined to pull you back. These same people seem to run at top speed to pour water on your flame of desire to reach higher in your pursuit of excellence.

They will tell you that your goals are *unrealistic* because they don't feel they could "pull it off." I like to call these people "dream vaporizers because they want to make sure your dream *vanish* into thin air.

If you are in the company of visionaries or people who sincerely want to make a difference in this world, they can identify your strengths. They can help you move toward your mission in life.

What kind of people do you attract? What is your greatest asset?

Make a list of personal friends who are passionate about life and spend prime time with them. That's where you'll get most of your encouragement and great ideas. I'm not saying that you should stop talking to cynical people; they too have great ideas. They also have their own *special* dose of encouragement that can be just as beneficial.

I'm just reminding you that your time is very valuable. You're on an important mission. Use your time wisely. A billion dollars can never replace each second that is wasted!

Find others whose goals match yours and see how you can help stretch their abilities. Look for ways to help others with their dream. Good deeds will always come back to you.

Join positive organizations such as Toastmasters, Rotary or Kiwanis, National Speakers Association, Big Brothers/Big Sisters, American Business Women's Association, or your local Chamber of Commerce. Become a volunteer for the Boy Scouts or Girl Scouts or any other group that gives you an opportunity to inspire others.

Start your own support group of people who will get together twice a month over breakfast, lunch or dinner to encourage and support each other. If you are unable to meet on a regular basis, send cards, letters or make phone calls to stay in touch and offer your assistance. But most importantly, be a person who keeps your word and find others who do likewise.

You Never Know Who You're Talking To

I heard Jim Rohn, a fellow professional speaker say these powerful words, "You never know who you're talking to." He was making reference to the fact that *everyone hasn't made it to where they're going.* Someone may be down on their luck today but swimming in the sea of prosperity tomorrow. You just never know. The most uncertain thing about life is . . . we don't know what the future holds for us nor do we know whose hand we will need to help us along the way.

I believe it is really in our best interest to sprinkle pieces of sunshine wherever we go.

You're an Ambassador

Whenever our ship, the USS Dwight D. Eisenhower would pull into a port, our captain could be heard on the ship's 1MC (loudspeaker) . . .

"Hello gents, this is the captain speaking. Before we pull into port today, I want to remind you that we are ambassadors to the United States of America." His words always had the sound of royalty to them. They made me feel important.

After we had pulled into the port in France, I had the pleasure of skiing the French Alps. During my break from skiing all morning, I met a young lady and we began to converse.

"Where are you from?" she asked.

"The United States," I said. "What about you?"

"Oh, I'm from London," she gracefully replied. "What do you do?"

I thought about the words our captain had spoken, I then responded, *"I'm -- an -- ambassador."*

By this time one of her friends had walked up to join our conversation.

She exclaimed to her friend, "He's an ambassador, can you believe it!"

"Well . . . what kind of ambassador?" her friend asked as if to catch me in a tangled web.

I paused for a moment to get my thoughts together and then smiling to myself, I replied, "I'm a *'good will'* ambassador from the United States. I'm pleased to meet you!"

They were both elated of course.

My captain had taught me well. That statement alone helped me to remember the fact that not only did I have a duty to represent the U.S. Navy in a positive light, I also represented all of my fellow citizens in the United States.

No matter where we go or what we do, we are still a representation of our wives, husbands, children, grandparents, mothers, fathers, sisters, brothers, etc. Our decisions never affect us alone, there will always be others who will be in the line of fire. There will be those who will have to pick up the pieces of our carelessness. The people that we surround ourselves with will either keep us in the right lane or cause us to veer all the way to left. Again I ask, who's in your club?

Are you a good ambassador for your family?

www.sparkplug.net

SPARK PLUG
POINTS TO PONDER

1. It does not matter how much you read positive material or attempt to apply spiritual principles if you do not have character.

2. Who's in your club?

3. Understand that people are either doing one of two things. They're either pushing you forward or pulling you back.

4. Find other people who have lofty goals and see how you can help each other.

5. Always remember, "You never know who you're talking to."

"Nothing great was ever achieved without enthusiasm."

- Ralph Waldo Emerson

Chapter 8

Can You Use a
Good Bargain Today?

I believe many salespeople receive a sour welcome because the public has not been educated about the importance of their occupation. The sales profession can be characterized as one of many spokes in the 'big wheel' of economics.

It's hard to imagine a world without an aggressive salesperson. Nothing takes place unless a sale is made. We are *all* selling something. When you go into your boss' office to ask for a raise, it is in your best interest to display an attitude of confidence and know how to sell yourself and your accomplishments. You must sell your skills and dazzling personality if you're interviewing for a job. When you're in need of a loan to start or expand your business, you've got to know how to sell your ideas to the banker. Even when you're interested in capturing someone's heart, you often spend a great deal of time selling your wonderful attributes. So whether it's an idea, personality, car, a bar of soap, jumbo jet, or a million thumb tacks, no transaction takes place unless a sale is made.

Sell . . . Sell . . . Sell!

If you took a poll from the general public, no doubt you will find that most people prefer a *guaranteed* weekly, biweekly or monthly income. The thought of being on 100% commission is enough to send many people scampering for something they describe as "a little more secure." But I happen to enjoy working in the realm of possibilities. It forces you to understand the real meaning of exercising faith on a daily basis.

If you have the right market, call enough people, have a spark plug attitude, *know* your product, *believe* in your product, have a little patience and the guts to ask for the sale, you can be a winner.

A few years ago my wife was employed as a salesperson. She wasn't moving much merchandise and soon became discontent with her job. After she expressed her frustration, I gave her Og Mandino's book entitled, *The Greatest Salesman in the World*.

Within the next few weeks, her sales more than doubled just by reading the book and applying the principles. She also gained a new level of confidence and greater respect for people in the sales profession. The best reward was the fact that she had a better attitude about her work and looked forward to breaking records each day!

One of the best books ever written about sales is a book by Tom Hopkins entitled, *How to Master the Art of Selling*. It is one of the most thorough books on the ' art of selling' that I've ever read.

No one is born a good salesperson. Everything that I have learned and mastered in sales was absorbed from a book, a seminar or my many years of sales experience.

Joe Salesman . . . That's My Name

Once upon a time, I worked for a thriving, California-based, neon sign company that had a branch office in Atlanta,

Georgia. The company specialized in custom outdoor signs that would give businesses optimum advertising exposure.

All recently hired employees had to travel to Savannah, Georgia for some practice training in the field. When the moment arrived for me to exercise my newly acquired skills in selling, my first stop was Tybee Island. I was very excited about driving down to see if I could sell some signs in that little area on the outskirts of Savannah.

After scouting around, I decided to stop at a nearby lawnmower repair business to sell the owner a brand-new, decorative, sophisticated sign. (It seemed as if Mr. LawnCare was overdue for a change in his image.) As I entered the shop, he was writing a check out to a young lady from the local Chamber of Commerce.

I knew Mr. LawnCare was either in a buying mood or he would tell me to get lost. Since I really needed the money, I prayed and asked God to let him be in a buying mood.

We exchanged greetings and made a little small talk. He was one of the many friendly people I met that bright sunny day in the cozy beach town of Tybee Island.

I made my pitch and proceeded to ask for the close. Immediately, Mr. LawnCare began to have some trepidation about buying the sign.

He was ranting about the fact that I had to have the check made out to me and I also had to go to his bank the same day to cash it and get a money order or cashier's check. I have never forgotten what he said to me after I told him what I needed to do.

He howled, "Let me get this straight! You're selling signs in Tybee Island today. The company you work for is out of California. You're from Atlanta, and you're training out of Savannah. You have a Florida tag on your car and you want me to write this check out to you so you can go across the street to my bank and cash it so you can get a cashier's check?!" At that point I paused and calmly agreed, "Yes sir, that's exactly what I want you to do."

I walked out with a smile on my face and the check in my briefcase. My prayer was answered. I'm glad Mr. LawnCare trusted his instincts.

As far back as I can remember, I have been a salesman. My earliest recollection of sales success was back in the seventh grade at St. Andrews Junior High School in Columbia, South Carolina. I sold more magazines than any of the students in the school and won a stereo set and other prizes. The next year in the eight grade, I outsold all of the other students again and won a trip to Carowinds, an amusement park situated on the South Carolina, North Carolina border.

In high school, when it came to talking my way out of trouble for eating candy in class, I acted as my own defense attorney. Mr. Cannon, the assistant principal, at Columbia High School in Columbia, South Carolina told me that I had a *gift* of persuasion. He then added that hopefully one day I would use my unusual gift to persuade people in a positive manner. I was always a talker, I always thought I had something to say.

Upon graduation from high school, I went off to Newberry College. Being the great salesman that I am, I sold myself to the freshman class and was nominated freshman class president.

I ran a very personable campaign and consequently won by a landslide.

After Newberry College, I moved to Atlanta, Georgia. My first job was at Captain D's where I worked as an assistant manager for a while.

Since face-to-face selling had always been my passion, I went to work with a company that required me to sell pots and pans, stereos, crystal wine sets, steak knife sets, plates and any other knickknack you can think of from the trunk of my car.

Hear me when I say this, "This job really tested my tolerance for pain and helped me develop inner strength!" There were days when hunger became an unwelcomed guest.

I would drive around yelling to potential buyers from

behind the wheel of my car, "Hey, ma'am . . . sir, can you use a good bargain today?!" I know the people thought I was a weirdo on the loose. There were many who didn't hesitate to snarl and tell me to 'beat it' while calling me all sorts of names I'd like to forget. Nevertheless, I understood their prudence. But there were also some who were hospitable and agreed to look at what I was selling. It was a very humbling experience but I will be eternally grateful for it! I learned a lot about humanity.

My next job was at Athletic Attic in Atlanta, Georgia. I was the top salesman of the month several times out of 250 stores. By the time I got promoted to store manager, we had bought our way out of Athletic Attic and changed the name to Sports' A Foot. (The owner of the store, John Smith, was responsible for giving me the moniker "Spark Plug" because of my inexhaustible energy and enthusiasm.)

I was very excited about getting promoted to manager because it required attending the managers' meetings in Colorado. It gave me an opportunity to snow ski in Copper Mountain!

After two years with Sports' A Foot I joined the Navy to continue to broaden my experiences while proudly serving my country. Traveling to countries such as France, Italy, Africa, South America, England, Spain, Turkey and Monte Carlo really helped me gain a new perspective on life and gave me a greater awareness and appreciation for different cultures.

I remember one custom I really liked in Italy; if a gentleman wanted to date a young lady, he would first take her mother a gift. I don't know why they follow this custom but I think it's because if the lady is not interested in the guy, the mother can be the defense attorney for him — who knows?

I got a chance to go to Rome, and visit Buckingham Palace in London. During my last year in the military, I ended up in Operation Desert Shield. We happened to be in the fifth month of a six-month deployment when Iraq invaded Kuwait.

The Navy really expanded my world view! Books became a constant friend when I was on six-month cruises. I also became a Big Brother with Big Brothers/Big Sisters of America.

My little brother was twelve at the time. (Ishmael is twenty-three years old now!) Time really does fly. He's married and I'm still in contact with him and his new family.

I developed a deeper appreciation for living in this country just by visiting other countries. America has so much to offer that we are often *overwhelmed* by the opportunities that lie before us. I also learned to be truly thankful for modern conveniences that so many take for granted.

There's Power in Believing!

It was the latter part of 1991. After five years of serving my country in the Navy, I began working at a local health club selling memberships. After a while, the challenge faded like a pair of worn out jeans. I began to think about leaving the company to seek other employment.

It just happened that our general manager at the time was demoted and transferred to another club. Since the new general manager who filled the vacancy was known to be the best salesman in the history of the company, I decided to stay on at the club. I had an opportunity to learn from a "sales pro."

Our new manager had never worked at a club that did not make quota. He immediately informed us that our club would not bring disgrace to his spotless record. He was also a meeting fanatic. We had meetings in the morning, afternoon and evening.

On the 1st of December he ushered us into his office and announced, "Gentlemen, I'm going to tell you up front that you're not going to like me. As a matter of fact you're going to hate me. However, on the 10th and the 25th, you're going to love me." The 10th and the 25th were the days we were compensated for all of our hard work. "And finally," he yelled, "we *will* hit quota!"

On that day we discovered our quota was about $150,000 for the month of December. Up to that point, we never knew anything about the quota. Our past general manager was very laid back so we all went with the flow and just did what we thought was a good job.

Our new manager's prophecy quickly came to pass. He was not our favorite person. He was also right about us paying homage to him on payday. Our payroll checks showed a *dramatic* increase which resulted from becoming more disciplined in our work.

Well, as the weeks roared by, he was still shouting, "We *will* hit quota! I don't care how you do it. Whether it's your mother, father, roommate, shipmate, sister, brother or friend that you sign up, I don't care," he yelled. This was a totally new concept for all of us. We stared at him as if he had just descended from the planet URCRAZY.

Finally, we all begin to feel the pinch because our time was running out. There were only three (3) days left in December and we were about $40,000 away from our quota. He called us into the office and gave us one of his motivational speeches about not giving up and he quoted Vince Lombardi.

My associates and I looked at each other as if to say to

ourselves, "This guy really believes we can hit quota." He refused to be counted out. He was pounding on his desk bellowing, "We will hit quota!" His management style was definitely one that could lead to high blood pressure.

I left his office saying to myself, "Maybe we *can* hit quota. If *he* really believes it, I guess we *can.*" From that day forward, I was determined along with my associates, to hit quota.

Well, on the last day of the year, December 31, 1991 it was going to be a short day at the club. Since it was New Year's Eve, instead of opening at 6:00 a.m., we opened at 8:00 a.m. We would normally close at 10:00 p.m. but today we were closing at 4:00 p.m. He called us into his office that morning and told us we had to make $20,000 in order to reach our goal. In the back of my mind I was saying to myself, "I've never seen this club do that much business in one day." However, at that point in the game, we could not rely on the facts. The *facts* were not going to help us reach our goal.

I will never forget that last day. By the close of business at 4:00 p.m. on December 31, 1991, true to our boss' word of not bringing disgrace to his spotless record, we sold over $25,000 in memberships! Our little club, the stepchild of the franchise with no pool or basketball court got the job done. Even though our club was the oldest and not the most glamorous in the franchise, we outsold every single one of the other health clubs in the city. I sold about three memberships that day. My friend Cecil sold a membership to his roommate.

Our general manager ordered pizza for everybody and we had a nice little pizza party to celebrate our victory. That was one of the most exhilarating feelings that I had ever experienced. Eventually, we all refused to lose, we chose to work as a team, and we hit quota! We proved to ourselves that anything is possible if we first believe. But it could not have been done if our general manager had not instilled the *power of believing* in his crew.

My Biggest Sale Ever

My life changed dramatically when I met Jacqueline who would later become my wife. I saw her walking across a crowded parking lot. The wind was blowing through her hair. She seemed to be floating on air and was smiling as if she had won a million dollars. There was music in the air and I was overwhelmed by her presence. Everything automatically went into slow motion like a scene from a movie. *Just joking.*

I saw Jacqueline walking across a parking lot and she *did* have a beautiful smile. I later learned she was doing some last minute shopping with her cousin before going on a trip to Bermuda.

After seeing her, I said to myself, "This will be my future wife." I began to wonder how I might be able to meet her. I knew if I didn't try to meet her at that moment, I'd never see her again.

I was also traveling with *my* cousin. He suggested that leaving a note on their car should do the trick. (I had seen them come toward their car, turn around and go back into the store because they had forgotten something.) Even though I had never tried to meet anyone this way, I gave it a shot. I didn't have much time left!

As I began writing, they were leaving the store again and approaching the car. I had to quickly finish writing the note and get it to her in time.

I barely made it. She had already opened the car door, sat down, and was just about to close it when I ran over, said 'hello' and handed the note to her just as a runner quickly passes a baton. *"Excuse me, I'd like to give you this. There's a note on the back,"* I added.

It was straightforward and simply written; "To the young lady in the black and white dress - if you are single, I would like to have lunch with you as soon as possible." I had written it on the back of my business card.

She called me that same night to let me know she would be on vacation for a week or so and she would call me when she returned. She did call me when she returned and of course the rest is history. True story.

I would not be where I am today without the support of my beautiful and talented wife. We have definitely experienced the power of "two." She has taught me to be more understanding of others and have more compassion for them. She has also given me some of the most brilliant ideas to help our company grow.

Jacqueline is definitely my inspiration and a gift from God. She is the spark of my life!

Our belief system has to be increased gradually. It is strengthened by taking action on small things which flourish and grow into enormous things. A castle can only be built by manually positioning one stone at a time.

Initially, I did not believe my general manager when he proclaimed we would reach our quota. But as he continued to instill this belief in us, it raised our level of expectation and expanded our possibilities!

1. We are all selling something, talents, skills, abilities, etc.

2. If you have the right market, call enough people, have a spark plug attitude, *know* and *believe* in your product and have the guts to ask for the sale, you can become a great sales person. It's that simple.

3. No one is born a good salesperson. It is a gift that can be acquired.

4. Our belief system is strengthened by taking action on small things which flourish and grow into enormous things.

5. Keep in mind that people ultimately buy you, your personality and your attitude.

"Why not go out on a limb? Isn't that where the fruit is?"

- Frank Scully

Chapter 9

Catch the Vision

Everything begins with a dream or an idea. On occasion, people actually *stumble* upon a great idea or invention that changes the course of history.

A flick of the switch to turn on your lights, start your car, computer, or washer and dryer -- all these modern conveniences started with an idea or a dream.

It takes a spark plug attitude to hold on to your dream. I have a deep appreciation for stories about people who held on to their dream and never let go regardless of countless setbacks and disappointments. Numerous biographies have been written about the courage of those who literally changed the world and set it on a new course.

I often think about Ronald E. McNair who was interested in science fiction as a young child and became one of NASA's shining stars. Though his life, along with six other colleagues was shortened by the *Challenger* explosion in 1986, he left a legacy of *courage*, *inspiration* and *excellence!*

My good friend, Carl McNair Jr, a successful businessman and founder of the Ronald E. McNair Foundation in Atlanta, Georgia, keeps his brother's dream alive by traveling around the country, encouraging other young people to pursue a career in math and science.

Al Mead, a gentleman I had the pleasure of meeting recently had to have his left leg amputated at a young age. He told me once that even though he lost his left leg as a child, he *breaks records* with his right leg. In the 1988 Paralympic games in Seoul Korea, he won a gold medal and set the world record in the long jump!

Kmart laughed at Walmart's founder, Sam Walton, and said he wouldn't last six months. Who's laughing now?

Mr. Rogers' show didn't get picked up by one of the major networks because they told him that anyone hosting a children's show must wear a costume. Three hundred Public Broadcasting Stations carry his program.

Cason and Virginia Callaway had a vision. In 1952 they founded Callaway Gardens near Pine Mountain, Georgia. Mr. Callaway, a millionaire textile manufacturer from La Grange, Georgia and his wife left a legacy for all of humanity.

There's enjoyment for the whole family. A 349-room inn, cottages, luxury villas, seven restaurants, a golf course, miles of hiking and biking, the largest tropical butterfly conservatory in the country, a beach, the world's largest collection of cultivated azaleas . . . just too many breathtaking sights to mention all sitting on 14,000 acres! My wife and I consider it to be our favorite hangout.

It has been proven that if you hold on to your dreams long enough, they can become a reality. If you forsake the doubters, work hard, work smart, find a mentor, balance your personal and spiritual life, you cannot and will not be denied.

My dream was to travel around the globe, sharing with others how attitude can considerably affect the quality of their lives. I wanted to help them realize they can literally *add a spark* to *whatever* they do! Through much prayer, pain, hard work, commitment, a spark plug attitude, and loving what I do, it has *finally* paid off.

Faith

Faith is believing in something even though you have no evidence! It acts as a power booster during times when you feel as if you've taken all that you can handle.

Faith requires that you wait patiently for something while being confident of the fact that it will be brought from the invisible to reality. You don't know when or how it will occur, you just know it is bound to happen — it's just a matter of time.

Are you *sitting* on great ideas that are stirring within you?

Are you still waiting for your life to *begin*?

If you are waiting for everything to be just right before you decide to catch the vision, it will never happen. Why should God trust you by giving you everything you need if you are not willing to use the little that you have?

My wife's grandmother always said, "The only time everything is going to be *straight* for you is when you're lying straight out in a casket." I know you're not going to pass up an opportunity to cast your ideas into the universe.

In order to exercise faith, you've got to do something. Merely talking about what you would like to do is not faith, but doing something when you don't know what to do--now that's faith! Taking action on something when you don't know whether it will work is a demonstration of faith.

Faith gives us the fuel we need to continue life's journey through both pleasant and not so pleasant experiences.

Always Expect a Host Miracles!

At our house and in our business my wife and I have an attitude of expectation when it comes to miracles or special occurrences in our daily lives. We *expect* something special every single day.

In addition to being thankful for the many activities most of us take for granted such as being able to rise on our own, breathe without medical assistance, feed and clothe ourselves, have a sound mind, and go where we choose, etc., we keep our *eyes peeled* for miracles because we know the world is full of them.

For us, every Friday is 'Good Friday' because it happens that most of our miracles occur on Fridays. We have come to expect extraordinary things on that particular day. Remember, you often get what you expect.

We have heard from a long lost friend, solved a multitude of problems, gotten a much needed word of encouragement, closed some of our biggest deals, received checks unexpectedly in the mail or a phone call with a *great opportunity* on that magnificent day. Though Fridays are special to us, we still expect something *extraordinary* every single day, all day long and all year long.

The best way to begin to raise your level of expectation and activate your creativity is to experience more, read more, learn more, do more, and *give more*. You'll find that the world will begin to open up like the delicate petals of a rose.

Go ahead . . . raise your level of expectation. Expect miracles. *They are freely given!*

SPARK PLUG
POINTS TO PONDER

1.   Everything begins with a dream or an idea.

2.   All the conveniences we have today were merely a dream in someone's mind.

3.   It has been proven that if you hold on to your dreams long enough, they can become a reality.

4.   Faith is believing in something even though you have no evidence!

5.   In order to exercise faith, you've got to do something.

"Do it trembling if you must, but do it!"

- Emmet Fox

Chapter 10

Fear…Don't Let It Get the Best of Everything!

Fear is the absence of faith. It is an enemy to our right to live an abundant life. Fear steals our opportunities and often causes illnesses of which the doctor can find no cure. It can drive us to destroy our own lives through terrible acts of suicide. Fear will persuade us to travel through this life without leaving a trail.

Of course there are some ways fear can benefit us, such as its use as a means of protection in dangerous situations. However, the fears I'd like to punctuate are the ones that keep us *immobilized.*

How can we combat this force which is the source of many undesirable results? We literally fight fear with one fist while we hold the other one in the air proclaiming there is no fear.

Getting rid of *debilitating* fears will often require you to get to the root of the problem in order to make some progress. The root of the problem is simply your attitude about you, your life and your world. Everything you believe to be true about yourself will be manifested through your actions. When you fail to change your attitude, your fears will multiply. Negativity attracts negativity.

If you believe you are incapable, you are. If you believe you must remain poor, you will. If you believe the whole world is a mockery, then it will be. If you believe there's no more goodness left in humanity, there won't be. Until you change your attitude, you cannot move in the direction of changing your life.

Failure Is Not Final

Who convinced you that you were a failure? You just might discover it was *you*. A judge will hear all the allegations and consider the evidence before a decision is made. They're the one who hands down the sentencing. In your private world, you are the judge. Why sentence yourself to a long life of fear, disbelief, sadness, lack of confidence and complacency? Make some positive decisions on your behalf. It may not be easy but it's possible!

Will you continue to sulk or decide to get up, get back in the game and go for the gold?

Trade your frown for a smile, your lack of confidence for boldness, your doubts for a strong belief in mighty miracles, your complacency for action and your fear for faith.

More than anything else, failure only denotes the inability to achieve (according to *your* standards) a successful outcome or result. Yet we have a tendency to embrace this word and allow it to define our entire being. We are not failures, we are people who sometimes don't get what we want. An optimist once protested, "You're not a failure if you don't make it-- you're a success because you tried." In trying, a result always occurs whether it's favorable or not so favorable. A valuable lesson can be learned from either outcome.

Nobody Likes Rejection

No one is seeking to be rejected. We all want someone to

affirm who we are and see us as what we could become. Our desire to find approval began in our families, the grass roots of our existence. If we did not receive it there, we usually went looking for it in other places. But an appreciation or approval of your identity can only come from inside. Taking the time to discover your true worth as a human being can often keep you from constantly wallowing in the muddy pool of fear and rejection. Changing how you think about your uniqueness and the reason you're on this earth can really make a difference!

Go Easy on Yourself

There's no need to spend time looking for an excuse or berating yourself because you didn't get the job, close the deal, make the team or whatever you were seeking. Sometimes someone else simply happened to get what you thought you deserved. Many times what we have to do is discover other creative methods, become more skilled or work harder and even smarter to accomplish the same goal. And then there are those times when we don't get what we want because divine order helps us wait for something *better* just around the corner.

Refuse to fall into the trap of believing that everything you attempt to do *never* works. It is merely an evil deception that has become a part of our thinking. The mind can be a playground for negativity. It has a tendency to keep you so wrapped up in the last negative episode of your life that you don't believe you can ever move forward.

At one of those times in my life when frustration had gotten the best of me, I read something by Arnold Schwarzenegger that stirred by soul. He stated, "Strength does not come from *winning*. *Your struggles* develop your strengths. When you go through hardships and *decide not to surrender*, that is strength."

Often after my presentations I would usually spend a good deal of time kicking myself around. "You forgot to say this, you forgot to say that, you should have said it this way or that way. Did the people have a good time?" Or when the audience evaluated my presentation and the final result was 99% success and 1% so-so, I could only focus on the 1%.

I finally decided that I would just try to be a conduit of inspiration. Now my attitude is . . . "If I was able to add a positive spark to at least one person's life in the audience, then my presentation was not in vain." This decision relieved a tremendous burden. I began to focus more on uplifting and encouraging my audience rather than wasting valuable time on petty doubts.

Concentrate on The Next Time

See yourself winning the battle that is ahead! Can you see yourself being victorious regardless of the outcome? And why are you victorious? Because you tried and you endured. You gave it your best shot!

Past disappointments are not always future predictions. Begin to let your attitude be one that exemplifies a true champion and you cannot be denied. In so many words, someone once commanded that we should "Walk like a champion, talk like a champion, train like a champion, think like a champion and we will *be* a champion."

It's all up to you. It doesn't matter what the record says. This is a new day. You are stronger and much wiser when it comes to handling anything that comes your way. Keep trying until you receive the results you are seeking.

After one of my *Overcoming Your Fears* presentations, one of the participants approached me with tears in her eyes. She confessed, "You know, three years ago I lost over $80,000 in my previous business. Until now, I really thought I was a failure. I had allowed that particular experience to negatively direct my life. Your message was a message of freedom for me; I *am not* a failure."

Since the young lady had lost a rather large sum of money, she lost confidence in her abilities. She buried her chances of every trying again because she could not bear the pain of another loss.

No experience can be trivialized because the results are all the same. People are left with a sense of worthlessness, a feeling of failure. Usually this feeling is carried around as one would carry a baby nestled in their arms. For some, this spirit of hopelessness is never released and they never, never *try* again.

Most often we want to complain about what we are unable to do or what has brought failure to us in the past. This only comforts us and gives us an excuse to remain where we are. Rising or getting up and moving on requires responsibility that we are not ready to take on. Even though we may proclaim that we want more out of life, we usually shy away from all the responsibilities which come with the package.

It's Never, Never Too Late

Society's definitions of success and wealth have caused many people to feel like failures. But that's not who *you* are and that's not who you were born to be. It does not matter where you are at this stage of the great game we call 'life', as long as you have breath in your body, there's an opportunity to accomplish whatever you desire! The game is not over until you breathe your *last* breath.

Don't be afraid of anyone trying to steal your idea, it cannot be stolen because no one will ever be able to operate like you can. No one has the same level of creativity that you have. Your age is no obstacle. Learn a new language, continue your education, write a book, train for a marathon, or do whatever you want. Don't put it off any longer, begin now!

Someone once revealed, that "Superiority and inferiority are born out of fear." The majority of us are fearful. We tiptoe through life with a hidden desire to *safely* make it to our grave without disturbing anyone. The baggage of fear weighs so heavily upon us that we never follow our heart.

Begin to *m-o-v-e!* Get up close to the monster, stare it in the eyes and it will begin to disappear. It will remain the big bad destroyer if you never face it. Children will always be afraid of the dark if you don't help them grow accustomed to it or change their attitude about it. The bully will always be the bully unless you make it known that you are not afraid.

What fears are weighing you down today? Begin to bench press them one at a time by *taking action* on the things you fear. You will gradually see fear hide its ugly face of defeat so that you can breathe freely and begin to move forward.

As I was driving around downtown Atlanta one spring day, my wife and I happened to see a young boy about six years old crouched at the curb on one of the busy streets. He was slowly looking both ways at the traffic, turning his small head from side to side as if he was watching an interesting tennis match. People seemed to be everywhere but no one acknowledged his presence.

I stopped and parked the car so I could find out why he was sitting there all alone. He was too young to be without adult supervision.

As I approached him, I stooped down beside his miniature frame and asked, "How are you doing, little man."

"*F-i-n-e,*" he slowly replied.

"What are you doing here? . . .Do you need any help?" I patiently asked.

"I'm trying to . . . c-r-o-s-s the street" he responded with tears beginning to stream down his face.

As I looked at the busy traffic and all the other obstructions, it was almost impossible for the young boy to cross the street alone. He was too small. He wouldn't have been able to run fast enough-- no one would probably see him in time to stop the car. The reason he was without adult supervision that day is another story. He was on his way from school and the crosswalk did not provide an incentive for the cars to slow down. Everyone was in a big hurry!

I simply took the little boy by the hand and safely lead him across the street. He was immediately relieved and his fear was gone. I watched as he started running at top speed toward the open door of a house that was familiar to him, no doubt his own.

Adults are often like that little boy I helped across the street that spring day. We start toward our dream with excitement and enthusiasm. We begin to stumble along the way and start doubting our abilities. It gets a little scary and eventually we just crouch down on the sidelines of life becoming content with just watching our dream slowly fade away. We don't always have someone to help us to break out of the immobilization that fear has draped over us. So we just sit.

If you ever feel as though you're crouching down on the sidelines of life just watching it pass you by, don't be afraid to ask someone to help you get back into the game.

SPARK PLUG
POINTS TO PONDER

1. Fear is the absence of faith. It is an enemy to our right to live an abundant life.

2. Fear will persuade us to travel through this life without leaving a trail.

3. We are not failures, we are people who sometimes don't get what we want.

4. Nobody likes rejection.

5. Life is a journey, concentrate on the next time.

"It's easy to sit up and take notice. What is difficult is getting up and taking action."

- Al Batt

Chapter 11

Sitting on the Sidelines Is Not an Option!

Are you expecting to do something great with your life? Do you want to become an expert at what you do? If so, it will require sacrifice. Be prepared to devote precious time to whatever you yearn to do without totally neglecting your family.

If you read enough books on any subject or spend enough quality time doing any task you can become an expert. Repetition is the key. Make a solemn pledge to yourself to stay focused in spite of all interruptions that come to squander your precious time.

Loving what you do will make the sacrifice a little easier to bear, but nevertheless, it is still a sacrifice. It still requires concentrating on a task when you probably need to be doing something else.

It may require playing the piano four hours a day, singing five hours a day or studying six hours every evening. Whatever you decide to do has to be what you live, eat, and breathe. It must be evident in every decision you make and every step you take. Are you willing to pay the price? Have you counted up the cost?

What Are You Waiting for?

Whether your dream is to become a great teacher, leader or the manager of your department, you must get up and move toward your goal. Of all the topics I have discussed, they are powerless unless action is taken. Action requires responsibility and decision making. Do not wait around for someone else to get the job done, take action. Action is the only path that leads to effective change. Research has shown that 85% of the people in America are not action oriented. They are just sitting on the sidelines, hopelessly waiting for success to fall from the sky into their arms. You *must* do something.

Most people are so overwhelmed with making a decision that they make no decision. Eventually their dream becomes so impotent that they forget how to dream. Believe that whatever decision you make is the *right decision.* Don't worry about making a *wrong decision,* go ahead and *take action.* Too many people have allowed great opportunities to pass them by because of their fear of making a bad decision.

Look around and evaluate others who are living life to the fullest. You will realize that these people are not particularly the brightest individuals but they are ones that merely took action on whatever they wanted to do.

Not only did they overcome inertia but they applied 'faith and works' which are a perfect mix for moving toward your goal. They just made up their minds to take action and stay in the race. *You've got to move.*

The main reason people find themselves sitting on the sidelines is because of doubt and fear. Even the great prophets and patriarchs of old had to deal with the fear factor. Moses, Jeremiah, Joshua, Gideon, etc., all of these mighty men of valor had to deal with trepidation. But they moved in spite of their fear.

A lack of confidence can paralyze us in such a way that we believe our dream is not worth the effort. We are afraid of what others might say or think because often our dreams begin to seem insurmountable even to ourselves. We eventually get stuck in the midst of our dream and attempt to humor ourselves by saying, "Oh, it probably wouldn't have worked out anyway" or "I guess it wasn't God's will." Take responsibility, fold up your tent and *start moving*.

Purpose in your heart that you are going to take the first step. Perfection is a mirage that will prevent you from moving at all. Just *make a start* toward your vision. My good friend and fellow speaker, Robert Davis has written a great book called *Implement Now, Perfect Later*. If you start now, the details *will* come.

Move now, get up now, commit now, take action now! It may involve talking to someone who is already doing what you would like to do, going to the library or surfing the Internet to get more information.

As you begin to take that first step, and I'm sure you will, it does not matter whether or not you see any results immediately. The most important thing is that you are moving. You have decided to stop hanging around the edge of life's ocean of possibilities and launch out into the deep. Most often, that which you are seeking is already waiting for you. Could you be late for your appointment? Don't let another moment slip away.

1. Be prepared to devote precious time to whatever you yearn to do without totally neglecting your family.

2. Becoming an expert is a statistical event.

3. Perfection is a mirage that will prevent you from taking action.

4. As you begin to take that first step, it does not matter whether or not you see any results immediately.

5. Take the first step today!

"Life is at its best when it's shaken and stirred."

- F. Paul Facult

Chapter 12

Service is an Attitude

Guess who works in every single department in the world? That's right, people. People who often have poor attitudes. They sit around as if they're outdated, worn out furniture and cramp the style and image of the whole company. Every business has a unique personality and it's usually made up of the 'spirit' of the *people* who work there.

If you mention the word *'service'* to some people, they would probably equate it to being in a restaurant or any other place where service is generally given.

But what about your contribution? Are you service oriented? Are you constantly on the lookout to find out how you can better serve your clients, customers, family, or mate? Do you live to make life easier for someone else?

Many would answer 'no' to all of the above. We prefer to be served rather than serve others.

What is it about service that automatically causes some people to skimp? Maybe they don't know that their livelihood, success of their business or the stability of their relationships could literally depend on how well they serve.

Remember, it's *all* attitude. If you made it this far into the book, it really shows your willingness to improve in the area of human relations. Congratulations!

At Christmas time do you run to the mall to buy gifts for people with poor attitudes? Unless you have matured in this area, you probably just give them a fruitcake and call it a day.

Does this scenario sound familiar? You are at the checkout counter buying Christmas gifts for your co-workers . . . "This is for Stephanie, this one is for Jacob, oh, Janice will really like this one, I'll give this one to . . . uhhh, oh no, let me put this back, I won't get this for Diane, she's got a bad attitude! Besides, after all I've done to help her with her late projects, she was never available when I really needed her to come through for me. I'll see what I can find for her in the Dollar store."

Think about this example . . . the Human Resource

department is seriously considering three highly qualified candidates for a promotion. The Human Resource manager informs the panel that Britania, Melinda and Jonathan are the leading candidates. Most certainly, without a doubt, Melinda has the most experience.

The chairman of the department immediately responds . . . "Well, can we eliminate Melinda right now?" (Everyone gasps.) "I know she has the most experience on the job but she also has a bad attitude. I've gotten too many complaints about her. She's too hard to deal with . . . I *don't* want to work with her and I don't want her to run our clients away. Now, *who* are those *other* candidates you were talking about?"

Sorry folks, this is reality.

I was in a bank about 15 years ago (I remember it as if it was yesterday) standing patiently in line to withdraw some money from my checking account. The young man who was in front of me boldly walked up to the counter and gave the teller the necessary information. She quickly punched his account number into the computer, read his current information and loudly responded in a hot scorching tone. . . .

"It would be **IMPOSSIBLE** for me to give you $20 out of your account when you only have $2.27 available!"

Needless to say, I wanted to crawl under rock. And if I wanted to crawl under a rock, who knows how that poor guy felt.

Embarrassment was an understatement! If he ever makes a million dollars, guess where he *won't* be taking his money.

I was doing business with another bank and just happened to go to a branch that had recently opened. As I slowly drove up to the teller window, I noticed the young lady had a scowl on her face.

"Whatever happened to service with a smile?" I asked.

"Oh, well-- I did that last week at the grand opening," she sneered.

Her reply was too ridiculous to address. Would the CEO run his company this way? I don't think so. The success of any business primarily depends on giving the people what they want. Generally, it works this way . . . the more people you can efficiently and adequately serve, the happier your customers will be, they will share their happiness with more people and you will make more money. Simple, right?

I never get any pleasure from patronizing businesses where I dread dealing with the people. Life already has enough challenges.

Just ask your kids which teacher they enjoy the most and I will guarantee it's usually the teacher with a great attitude. It's usually the teacher who has enthusiasm and passion for what they are teaching. Students actually experience accelerated learning and retain more in this environment.

I remember a guy who literally rolled out the red carpet at an oil change business in Jacksonville, Florida. He was courteous, enthusiastic, and knew the value of good customer service. In addition to the oil change business, he also owned a carwash which was next door. Not only would customers get their oil changed but the fluids were topped off, the carpet vacuumed, and an air freshener placed in the car. And that's not all. You'd also get a packet of Armor All, a complimentary token for a carwash, and a lollipop. After all of this, you were out of the door in 10 minutes!

Now it's time for a pop quiz. What level of *service* do *you* get with your oil change?

After I moved to Atlanta, I was planning my visits back to Jacksonville, Florida around the time I needed an oil change!

When you take the time to go above and beyond, people notice. It has also been proven that people who have discovered the *joy* of serving others are actually healthier individuals.

Many years ago, when I was about 21 years old, I was visiting one of the nursing homes in Orangeburg, South Carolina. It was around October, just about the end of the year. (Today my wife and I still get joy out of our weekly visits to the nursing home in our community). I was going from room to room saying 'hello' to the residents.

Some of the elderly ladies would yell out "Junior, is that you?!" I would reply, "No ma'am, it's not Junior, my name is Anthony and I'm just stopping by to say hello."

I'll never forget the resident in the last room I visited that chilly day in October. It was evident that the lines in her face were a diagram of the years of sadness and disappointment that she had endured. I sat and talked with her a while.

As we finished sharing a few bits and pieces of small conversation, I was about to walk out the door when she slowly reached out her frail hand and beckoned for me to come near to her. Holding my hand in hers, she whispered, *"I just want to thank you for visiting with me today because y-o-u are the only visitor I've had all year."*

We waste no time getting rid of everything old in our lives. Old shoes, old dresses, old furniture, old cars, etc., are thrown away and we do the same to the elderly. We often forget to serve them by giving a little of our time.

It was Ralph Waldo Emerson who said "The *only* gift is a portion of thyself."

Can You Teach Me How To Act Like I Care?

When I worked in the health club business, it gave me great pleasure to assist my clients in building a well-toned body. Some of them were bashful first timers so it required that I spend a little extra time familiarizing them with all of the exercise equipment.

Not only did I have to spend time giving them helpful workout tips, I also had to close a certain number of sales each day. So between personal training and recruiting clients, I organized my time very wisely and was ranked among the top sales people. Success did not come because I was a great time manager but because my existing clients often gave me referrals in exchange for exceptional customer service.

After some time, a fellow associate who had been studying my 'technique' walked into my office. He was one of those guys that the ladies raved about, a sort of Tom Cruise or Denzel Washington type. "Mr. Cool" never had any problems getting clients to sign up because most of the females flocked to him. Some of you know what I'm talking about.

Anyway, one day I was totally shocked when he stood in the doorway of my office and made a solemn request.

"Anthony," he said, "I've been checking you out for the past couple of weeks and you're really a great salesman. You're so good with the people. You act as if you really care about your clients and they seem as if they really like you."

"I was wondering . . . *can--you--teach--me--how--to--act--like--I--care*?"

I paused for a moment, looked at him in disbelief and slowly answered, "I'm sorry my friend . . . but that's something I *cannot* teach you. *It has to start inside.*" I could see him lose his composure in spite of his cool, calm demeanor. It was not the answer he was expecting. He was only looking for a new 'technique' to use on potential clients.

Though 'Mr. Cool" was popular in the business and could use his good looks and charisma to get the sale, he was clueless about exceptional customer service after the sale. Therefore, he was left with a high cancellation rate and plenty of unhappy customers who were not interested in sending him additional business.

Because my clients knew I cared, they willingly made my job easier by giving valuable referrals of roommates and others who eventually came to the club and signed up as a new member.

SPARK PLUG
POINTS TO PONDER

1.   "Service" is really all about attitude.

2.   Are you service oriented? Are you constantly on the lookout to find out how you can better serve your clients, customers, family, or mate?

3.   Generally, when you give people what they want, the happier they will be and the money will follow.

4.   It has also been proven that people who have discovered the joy of serving others are actually healthier individuals.

5.   Good service depends on the condition of your heart.

"Happiness is a perfume which you cannot pour on others without getting a few drops on yourself."

- Rabbi Louis Man

Chapter 13

Giving It
All You've Got

Are you honestly giving life all you've got?

How high is your aim and where is your target? Is your chin constantly dragging on the ground or are you setting your sights way above the ominous clouds?

As we have heard so often, "This life *is not* a dress rehearsal." We won't have another crack at precious time that washes away in a tidal wave of negativity. So, if you shoot for the stars, it won't matter if you hit the moon. Aim high. Be *determined* to walk above your circumstances and you'll *never* settle for the tattered shoes of defeat.

But before you aim high, be mindful of the 'little things' that may affect your aim.

High up on the list, *worry* and *fear* always lurks. Tomorrow manages to *grab* the present from us and yesterday *battles* for our attention. It becomes increasingly difficult to consistently aim high, keep our eye on the target and give life our best shot. We feel as if we must keep a portion of ourselves *on the shelf* for fear of losing something or someone as we climb the mountain. But *I* would rather die *trying,* even when it looks as if all hope is gone than to have never tried at all.

Age and aim are not synonymous. You're not too old. If your body is too mature to be a gymnast, learn about the sport so you can *teach* others and still be close to something that interests you.

Procrastination will affect your aim. Set out to do as much as you can *today* because this present second will never return. All the energy in the world cannot bind this day and put it in a bottle.

An attitude of gratitude can positively affect your aim. Take a moment to give thanks for being granted one more day to cherish life and the opportunity to aim high. Appreciate the ability to breathe in and out. If you are able to move around and go *anywhere* you choose, be thankful! Give thanks for the ability to think for yourself and make your own decisions.

Live Long & Like It

For twenty years my granny has been a member of *Live Long & Like It*, a positive organization that reminds people to celebrate life no matter how old they are. They take exotic cruises, attend monthly meetings, go to fancy dinners and experience many other exciting festivities.

Granny won't tell me her age but if I had to take a wild guess as to how old she is based on her energy, enthusiasm and love for other people, I would say she's in her 20's. She's about 4'9", beautiful, smart, has an eye for fashion and loves to laugh. She definitely gets the most out of life.

Whenever I'm in the mood to leisurely drive from Atlanta to Jacksonville, Florida to visit, it's protocol to let her know I'm coming because she just may out of town. (No surprises for her!)

Whether it's faithfully helping out at the church, taking care of her older sister, Ann, traveling around with her daughter Betty, participating in the social events of Live Long & Like It, or showing concern for others in the community, granny always has a full schedule.

As long as I've been visiting her, there's always one thing I can definitely count on -- my favorite, freshly baked, mouth-watering, flavorful, moist, homemade pound cake waiting for me. It's always the same delicious cake with a jumbo pecan topping. Each pecan is patiently shelled with her own hands and placed neatly around the top of the cake. A sweet, delectable, melt-in-your- mouth glaze lazily drips down the sides.

I've never tasted any other dessert that beats the richness my granny's cake. She makes each one with lots of loving care.

I'll always adore granny because of her loving spirit, and unbridled enthusiasm. The unconditional love she freely pours upon others will be a monument for everyone that have been graced by her presence.

Did you know that *scientists have long proven that the spark of life can be prolonged indefinitely?* It has also been revealed that those who follow their creative passions throughout their lives are happier, more active senior citizens.

This just may explain why some of our greatest painters throughout history created some of their best work near the end of their lives. Monet, Picasso, and Renoir's golden years were filled with creativity. Even the *great* Grandma Moses didn't start her creative career until she was past seventy years old.

Ms. Camille Winslow is 85 years old. I happened to meet

her one evening on the side of the road where unfortunately her car had stalled. She was on her way to a class at the Atlanta University Center.

As I was driving past, she had the hood of the car raised and was peering inside as if she was a trained mechanic.

I quickly thought to myself, "I certainly wouldn't want that to be *my mom* stranded on the side of the road." Instantly, I swirled around to see if I could be of any assistance.

"What's wrong — can I help you with something?" I asked.

"I really don't know" she replied.

I took a long look under the hood even though I knew I didn't know too much about mechanics. After tinkering with the gadgets underneath, I kindly asked, "Do you need me to drop you off somewhere?"

"Sure, if you don't mind," she said.

As we got into my car, she thanked me for my hospitality. She asked me about my home town. I told her I had just moved from Jacksonville, Florida where I was in the military for five years.

She also wanted to know how much I knew about the history of Atlanta. I informed her that I wasn't too familiar with the history so she proceeded to give me a brief tour.

As I was driving, she pointed out some of the historical

landmarks around the city and shared some interesting and valuable information about each one. After she had finished her role as a tour guide, I safely dropped her off at her house and we chatted for a while. She gave me her phone number and I promised I would stop by and visit occasionally to make sure she was O.K. I kept my word and visited her periodically.

I even took my fiancee to meet her before we got married. Five years later, Mrs. Winslow is still a wonderful friend. She has also adopted my wife.

Ms. Winslow amazes me because her mind is extremely bright and of course, there is a bounty of wisdom to share. She asks lots of questions and is an incredible conversationalist. A lover of history, politics, reading, exercise, and lively debates she also serves as a business consultant. Ms. Winslow is living long and loving it!

Are you following your creative passion or have you figured out what your passion happens to be? Michelangelo stated, "It is only well with me when I have a chisel in my hand."

Besides speaking, my passion is tennis. When I'm playing tennis, all seems right with the world. My wife and I also enjoy visiting the mountains. We've probably visited every mountain in North Georgia. The clean air, breathtaking beauty, low level of stress in the atmosphere and an abundance of trees is always just what the doctor ordered. When you do more of what you enjoy, it improves your attitude.

Passion is the mother of enthusiasm. What are you so passionate about that when you're doing it, all seems right with the world? What puts fire in your belly? If you haven't put your finger on it yet, keep thinking.

We Don't Need All the Answers But We Will Have The Answers We Need

Many things are still a mystery to us. We will never fully understand the death of innocent people, why some sicknesses are not healed or why things just don't seem to be working out as we would like. There are places in the universe where feet cannot tread, hands cannot reach and voices cannot be heard.

The Creator and Ruler has dominion. It is not necessary for Him to operate in a way for us to always understand what is happening in His world. Would you let anyone know *everything* that goes on in your house? However, one thing remains certain, God knows exactly what He's doing and His timing is perfect. Everything is being worked out toward the good no matter what it may be or how it seems from our bird's eye view of the world.

If you ever feel the need to complain, make an effort to visit a children's hospital. Gaze into the innocent eyes of those who live moment by moment in the shadows of a fatal illness. Hold the tender hands of the small burn victims and experience their courage to survive. Open your heart and listen to the silent scream of those who have experienced other kinds of trauma.

Visit a veterans' hospital and bear witness to a world of forgotten heroes. Some are without limbs. Many are suffering from 'mysterious' diseases. Others have given up hope.

Go to a nursing home and look into the lifeless eyes of those who never get visitors all year long.

Take the time to talk to the homeless men, women and children with broken spirits and shattered dreams.

Try to see if you can really have compassion for someone who is bedridden with jolts of excruciating pain.

Have a heart-to-heart talk with your next door neighbor. You'll find that your complaints will begin to vanish and you will feel the urge to kneel down and say a prayer for others who are in desperate need of physical and emotional healing.

Be thankful on a daily basis and always remember when you walk through the valley of the *shadow* of death, there is a divine blessing wrapped up in it!

Our greatest strength still lies in our ability to stand tall in the midst of despair and abandonment. The pain forces us to look within ourselves. It provides an opportunity for us to *grow* by leaps and bounds.

I have never heard anyone shout joyously about the rigors of boot camp. But I've heard them proclaim that the intense training conditioned their minds and their bodies to become good soldiers. So it is with life. If you can accept all experiences as training for the next promotion, you will be able to stay on course.

Learn to laugh in the unfriendly faces of discouragement and hate. Gird up your loins with inner strength during times of weakness and set aside some private time to rest your weary soul.

Do thoughtful little things for your children, mate, friends, and associates to surprise them and let them know how much you appreciate their presence in your life.

We are all still growing. We all need someone to tolerate us and exercise patience with our moods and attitudes. We need someone to listen to our cry when we are in pain without criticizing our weaknesses. We crave approval and we need to have the feeling that we belong. We all just need someone to remind us that we are special and our life matters!

The trials of life *are* blessings for us -- they're just of a difference species. Many triumphs have been hewn out of mountains that seemed insurmountable. Electrifying and profitable ideas have spilled out of a wounded heart. Breakthroughs have come when it seemed as if we have gone as far as we could go. The most potent seeds have been those planted through great affliction and sacrifice.

America is still the richest country in the nation. We live in a land where food is discarded by the truck loads. Forgotten clothing sometimes hang within our closets with the sales tag still attached. Shoes are a fashion statement. Department stores and restaurants abound like sands on the seashore. Abundance is as far as our eyes can see.

In this era, we are experiencing some of the most dramatic breakthroughs in science and technology that are too numerous to mention. Yet most of our time is spent murmuring and complaining. We cannot appreciate progress because we take practically everything for granted.

What are you taking for granted? What are you complaining about today? Do you think you'll ever be able to *celebrate* life?

Will you let illness or the death of a loved one be the ultimate wake-up call in your life? Norman Cousins stated so beautifully, "The tragedy of life is not death, but what dies inside while we are living." Has something died inside of you?

I've known Shannon since I was 12 years old. She was only in the first grade when her family became our neighbors in Columbia, South Carolina. I adopted her as well as her other siblings as part of my family. We literally grew up together.

Whew! It seems like yesterday! She was smart as a whip, always made straights A's throughout all her years of school. And not only was Shannon incredibly talented, she had a great personality!

"Shannon's sick. " Her brother was at the other end of the telephone receiver. "They're still doing some tests," he said.

I found her hospital room at the end of a long hallway in sterile surroundings. She was her usual jovial self.

Surprised that my wife and I had driven from Georgia to South Carolina just to pay her a visit, she got a little emotional and expressed her gratitude.

My wife and Shannon instantly hit it off and were laughing and talking like two old friends who couldn't wait to share a bit of good news.

"I'll be out of here in a few days," she said. "They're only running a few tests." She was definitely in a cheerful mood. "I'm just having a little trouble with my heart," she confided.

Shannon and I began to talk about the "good 'ole days." We talked about all the fun we had just running around the neighborhood with other kids. The simple things brought us joy in those days and if other parents saw the need to discipline us, they didn't hesitate. We had surrogate parents all over the community!

Summer was always the best time of the year because of the array of activities that were available — swimming, tennis, picnics, birthday parties, ball games, etc. Kids were all over the place just having a good time. Excitement and laughter were always in the air! We both had fond memories about our neighborhood in Columbia, South Carolina!

I had an opportunity to talk with 27-year-old Shannon on the phone about two months after visiting her. She had already been in and out of the hospital a few times since our last conversation.

As I spoke with her, I couldn't help remembering the little innocent six-year-old who played freely under the warmth of the sun. Our conversation reminded me of how precious good health is and how often we take it for granted. What she was about to reveal to me was heartbreaking.

"I have cancer of the heart," she said. "I have to be on oxygen 24 hours a day. The oxygen tank is beside my bed and when I leave the bedroom I have a portable tank which only has

a three-hour supply of oxygen. At one point, I had to have my throat cut and I have a tube in my nose 24 hours a day. I have to be in the hospital one week out of every month. The chemotherapy takes four days and I've lost all my hair. The blood transfusion takes twelve hours. I have a permanent I.V. in my chest and I've had three operations already. My medical bills are over $60,000."

"Yet . . . I still feel lucky to be here. There are more people that are worse off. If I had to live my life over again, I wouldn't worry about the petty things. They wouldn't get to me. I would enjoy life more and make better decisions. Ultimately, I wasn't running my life, life was running me."

I attended Shannon's funeral one month later. I was still working on this particular chapter of the book. It was the first time the reality of our bodies being an earthly house really struck me. When I viewed the cold, empty, lifeless framework of what was left of her, no one could convince me that it was Shannon. It was just a physical testament of the fact that she had walked this way . . . *only a shell.*

I know her spirit is at rest now. There is no more suffering in her body.

During the funeral services, close friends were asked to contribute warm words of remembrance about Shannon. They all shared how they were given courage to face the difficulties in their lives. She helped them re-evaluate what was really important.

I'm sure at times Shannon may have trembled with fear and uncertainty about her future and the well-being of her only son, but she still transferred the 'spark' of life.

I'll never see Shannon's smiling face again or hear her hearty laughter. I'll never be able to talk with her about the good 'ole days.

Nevertheless, her spark plug attitude will always be remembered. Her fierce determination will be forever etched in my memory.

SPARK PLUG
POINTS TO PONDER

1. It is not *important* for us to know how long we must endure our trials and tribulations.

2. The *most important* thing is what we become during the process of our afflictions.

3. Don't let illness or the death of a loved one be the ultimate wake-up call in your life.

4. We cannot fully appreciate progress because we take practically everything for granted.

5. When was the last time you gazed into the beauty of a clear blue sky or a starry night?

"*The surest path to happiness on this earth comes from losing yourself in a cause greater than yourself.*"

- Brendan Byrne

Chapter 14

Life: A Song Worth Singing

This short chapter is primarily written to remind you that *all things are possible for you!* I strongly believe in *practicing* the art of thinking in the realm of abundance and not lack; freedom and not bondage; love and not hate; peace and not war.

I believe in focusing on what's *possible* for me and my family. I refuse to sit by and just lazily accept what life hands me.

I once heard someone say "If you don't fight for what you want, you deserve what you get." You've got to be willing to fight for your future.

I know there is always more to achieve, more to experience and more to give because to think any other way is to work against the plan and purpose for my life.

Though you may not have a manifestation of things that are possible for you at this time, it doesn't mean it can't happen. Keep the fire burning. Keep creating a larger vision for your life by pushing beyond your doubts and fears. Stay alert for new ideas that can open up the windows of your soul. It would sadden me to know that you reached the end of your years without attempting to move beyond where you are at this moment and stretch your abilities. There are no limitations for you. If you have the desire, that's reason enough to know that you can accomplish whatever you set out to do.

Your mind is just too phenomenal to continue to be a cluttered dumping ground for thoughtless remarks and flimsy suggestions of others.

You are your own artist, you can paint your own picture. No one can paint it as colorfully and as creatively as you can. No one will have the same strokes on the canvas that you will put into motion. Your destiny only has *your* name on it.

There are times in all of our lives when we must be ready and willing to take a giant leap of faith. We've got to sometimes walk where there are no trails and journey into the forest alone.

Too often people give up and drop out of the race. Don't give up because as the great Shirley Caesar sings so beautifully, *"You may be next in line for a miracle!"* You may be close to crossing the finish line. But you'll never know it if you throw in the towel. You'll just live a miserable unfulfilled life. Not only so, you are depriving others of an example of triumph.

Each day we are all faced with a unique package of challenges. But there are multitudes of opportunities within each one of them. From the moment we arise out of bed, we begin to unwrap our personal package for the new day. Remember, we cannot focus entirely on the package (experience) itself; we can't afford to do so. It may cause us to miss what would otherwise bless our souls.

Don't always be so quick to run or retreat. There comes a time when you need to stand and refuse to give up on whatever you happen to working toward. Nevertheless, there are also times when you must retreat in order to survive or discover a new and effective direction. You've got to trust your own heart!

Sure the load gets heavy. Times get a little tough. The way gets a little bleak and at times it will be difficult to find support in your calling. You may find yourself asking the rhetorical question, *"Hey! What's it all about??!"*

You're *definitely* going to get weary and every once in a

while it may seem as if everything has come to a screeching halt.

Keep the faith!

Many of life's challenging experiences are just some of the perks of being a card-carrying member of the human race. Whatever you are experiencing, someone has already endured it and gone on to overcome many of life's hurdles. They were not superhuman. Divine intervention, grace, prayer, persistence, and a *spark plug attitude* were their keys to success.

We trust that you will continue your journey of discovering the benefits of having a *spark plug attitude*. It is stress medicine for your soul, comfort for your spirit, creativity for your work and powerful energy for your body.

Go ahead . . . get ready to face the day with confidence. Hold your head up! Pull your shoulders back. Believe the goals you have set for yourself are priceless and within your reach, because they are. They are certainly worth the struggle. You will surely find that unlimited opportunities await those who have discovered the awesome power of a *spark plug attitude!*

E-mail "The Spark Plug"
When You Visit
www.sparkplug.net

Jacqueline Thomas
Vice President of Ideas

Jacqueline, the *creative* force behind the success of Spark Plug International, has a degree in management and computer science. She is also a freelance writer, author, publisher, poet, consultant and presentation coach.

When she isn't hammering away at her computer, you just might find her enjoying her passion for reading, hiking in the mountains or meditating on new ideas.

Email: myideas@rocketmail.com

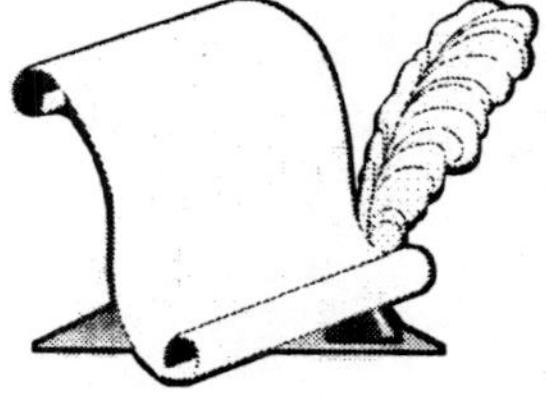

Order Form

Qty.   **Books**

______ Spark Plug Attitude *$15.00*

______ 125 Ways to Add a Spark to Your Day: *Living*
with an attitude of giving *$10.00*

T-Shirts
Specify Large or X-Large

______ It's All Attitude *(L or XL)* *$10.00*

______ Spark Plug Attitude *(L or XL)* *$10.00*

______ You Can Add a Spark to Whatever You Do *(L or XL)* *$10.00*

______ Spark Plug World Tour *(L or XL)* *$15.00*

Quote Pack *(Mini Poster Edition)*

52 Selected Quotes to Live By
______ (One for each week of the year) *$20.00*

Please allow 7 - 10 days for delivery. Make check payable to:
Spark Plug International
115 Windsor Circle, Fayetteville, GA 30215
(770) 964-1000
Visa/MasterCard Accepted!

Name____

                                          Phone No.

Address____
                    (Please Print Clearly)

Postage & Handling Charges

$5.00 - $10.00	3.00
$10.01 - $25.00	4.00
$25.01 - $50.00	5.50
$50+	7.50

Total Order

Total Merchandise + Shipping
(Write in Total Amount)
$_____________

*We Appreciate
Your Business!*